FROM FOOD STAMPS TO

Favor

...Created to conquer,
made to master, and
born to beat the odds!

Kandra C. Albury

Copyright © 2013 Kandra Albury
(Re-released April 2020)

All rights reserved. No part of this book may be used or reproduced by any means, graphic, electronic, or mechanical, including photocopying, recording, taping or by any information storage retrieval system without the written permission of the publisher except in the case of brief quotations embodied in critical articles and reviews. Copying this book is both illegal and unethical.

ISBN 978-1647-1368-95 (paperback)

Scriptures taken from the HOLY BIBLE, NEW INTERNATIONAL VERSION®. Copyright © 1973, 1978, 1984 Biblica. Used by permission of Zondervan. All rights reserved.

Published in the United States of America

Acknowledgements

This memoir is dedicated to the most amazing ghost writer I have ever encountered… the Holy Spirit; He is the presence that jogged my memory, and inspired line after line and detail after detail, and for this I am truly thankful. When I felt weary in the completion of this task, the Spirit gently whispered, *"Kandra, you must finish this work!"*

I am eternally grateful to my mom and grandparents for introducing me to the Holy Spirit when I was a child. It is because of God, that I believe every circumstance is surmountable because *His* love is unconditional and unfailing. So, thank you God for being my friend, my ever-guiding conscience, and my greatest inspiration.

If no one else believed in me, I know my husband James, children, and mother did [and always will]. I am confident that this literary work will reveal the radiance behind my smile and the resiliency of my spirit.

When I shared the title of this book with one of my dearest friends, she asked, "Who was on food stamps?" Her candid response served as confirmation for the title; authentic conquerors rarely look like what they've endured [God's Word promised beauty for ashes, Isaiah 61:1-3]. There is no greater feeling of triumph, than when you've truly survived the flames of life, and the residue is untraceable!

Thank you, Pastor Troy Rumore (Kelli), Pastor George Dix, (Lady Michele) and Pastors Carlos and Gerri Duffey for teaching that kingdom living isn't for the afterlife but for now. A special thanks to my Pastor Troy Rumore, Assistant Pastor Dwayne Thomas, you're appreciated more than you'll ever know. To some of my favorite televangelists Joel Osteen, Creflo Dollar, Joyce Meyer, Bishop T.D. Jakes, Joseph Prince and Juanita Bynum. There are several more, but I'll stop here. All of you have given me a timely word of grace while channel surfing.

To my husband, James, thank you for your continual prayers and support. I love you. To my children, you're loved and this work is a piece of my legacy. I love you all immensely, especially you Kenzy (my beloved grandson).

Additionally, I devote this work to those who have endured or are enduring rough economic times. Countless of you, for the first time, have found yourselves on governmental assistance to save your home or food stamps to put food on the table. My words of encouragement to you are to focus on at least two reasons to endure "the struggle;" one substantial reason for yourself and another reason for your loved ones. Whatever you do, don't throw in the towel! Hang on to it, wipe our face, and stay in the ring!

Remember, *your* fight is *fixed*, and the bookie is God! God sent His only son, *Jesus* who overpowered *Satan*, and today He [Jesus] still reigns heavyweight champion of the world! He defeated death, hell, and the grave in a single knockout!

Stick it out until you can sense the table turning in your favor. Remember this and say it loudly and proudly: "I am a child of God who was created to conquer, made to master, and born to beat the odds!"

"History shows us that recessions and other unfortunate situations are inevitable yet surmountable. History also teaches us there can be no victories without wars, no peace without chaos and no change without courage."

~Kandra C. Albury

TABLE OF CONTENTS

Foreword / 8
Introduction: Elementary Lessons, Realized Life Lesson(s) / 13
It was All Part of the Master's Plan / 22
Early Exposure Equals Life Composure / 53
When Your Pitstops Prepare You for Your Purpose / 64
Mentality Shift Equals Lifestyle Shift / 74
Pray for the F's and G's / 83
And It Shall Surely Come to Pass / 87
Favor Doesn't Exempt, It Qualifies / 91
Choose Love and Go Out of Your Way to Express It / 105
Trauma Produces Tenacity and Builds Our Faith / 110
Don't Scrub the Mission / 122
Take Time to Discover Your Gifts / 136
Forgiveness Isn't Optional / 147
Fear or Faith- You Choose / 157
Angels: Heaven's Ambassadors on Earthly Assignments / 166
Are You Kingdom-minded, Double-minded or Absent-minded? / 178
Sassy, Single, and Surely Worth Marrying / 186
Grace Is Yours and You Don't Have to Ask for It / 209
It Happened to You, but Refuse to Allow It to Ruin You / 219
From the Shore / 234
Healing Prayer for Victims of Childhood Sexual Abuse / 242
About the Author / 246

Foreword

Food Stamps to Favor... The beginning

"I am not saying this because I am in need, for I have learned to be content whatever the circumstances. I know what it is to be in need, and I know what it is to have plenty. I have learned the secret of being content in any and every situation, whether well fed or hungry, whether living in plenty or in want. I can do all things through him who gives me strength." Philippians 4:11-13, NIV

It's one thing to fall on hard times and another to be raised on hard times for 18 years. To be liberated from a lifestyle plagued by poverty requires answering these questions: "How can I make the most of this situation while I'm *here*? Secondly, is this the way I *want* to live my life for the rest of my life?"

I knew adhering to my mom's advice about getting an education would be my one-way ticket out of an impoverished lifestyle.

Transitioning from a lifestyle of scarcity to abundance, necessitates the expectation of unacceptance and not being respected (this *may* come at the end of each process). It requires accepting uncertainty and at times feeling lost in the shuffle of life, but with self-discipline and leaning on the God of the universe, victory is inevitable! Less than *your* best will never be good enough to some, but the reality is… pleasing "some" is not the *ultimate* goal because looking for *that* one person who will listen, act and believe in you will undeniably lead to disappointment. Our strength comes from within, OWN your God-given awesomeness! Abandon every excuse, go even when fear rears its head, and rise to the occasion of *your* greatness; be THE person you've been longing to encounter— YOU are the conqueror that God created you to be [Romans 8:37]!

Sometimes we are ashamed to talk about where we come from. Although, I am grateful for my humble beginnings, I, too, for many years was embarrassed by a poverty-stricken past but since my conscience (the Holy Spirit) kept nagging me, I knew it was time open the diary of my heart, and reveal what *was* my shame… but now I recognize it as my foundation of greatness. From poverty to prosperity [not financially, but purposefully and spiritually]; the discovery of my peace, callings, gifts, and purpose(s) in life. This expanded definition of joyous prosperity rests deep within the soul and remains unchanged by the certainties or uncertainties. Unlike happiness, which comes and goes, joy is constant despite the outcome. Joy allows me to relax in the confidence that God created me to soar, and there are eternal connections and benefits when I choose joy. Joy keeps the momentum going when happiness takes a sabbatical. When we master keeping a grateful heart during our mountain top and valley low experiences, it conditions us to be at peace *with* life because of God's sovereignty. Joy helps keep our emotions grounded by simply understanding that things could *always* be worse *or* better.

This exposure of my former life is embarrassing and irrefutably touché. However, these chapters of my life have also provided the drive and the willpower I *need* to master my present and future situations.

After reading this book, it is my hope that each reader will understand that downfalls are conquerable through God's perfect strength and immeasurable power.

When we tap into God's power, it revolutionizes our lives as well as the lives of others. When we reflect on our personal experiences and share our stories, we often discover truth, resiliency and perseverance through pain, challenges, tragedies and triumphs. When we own God's power, it empowers us to live our best blessed life and discover God's truth regarding us, time and time again.

The truth liberates and positions us to invite others aboard the freedom ride of life. When we share our truths, lives are changed by it. Once united with truth, no one can take it away or minimize it. When discovered, it becomes a precious jewel in our treasure box of life– it's invaluable and irreplaceable. Often times, truth serves as our passport to examine, advocate, disconnect, reconnect and confront. It empowers us to calm any storm or create one. *Truth is the light that enlightens*!

"And you will know the truth,

and the truth will make you free."

John 32:8, NLT

Elementary Lessons Realized Life Lesson

When I was in elementary school, I aspired to accomplish three things: To become a safety patrol officer, win big during our annual field day, and earn a treat from the teacher's treasure box daily.

The honor of being a patrol meant that I *could* lead. The triumph of a win during field day meant I *possessed* the strength and courage to overcome my opposition, and being chosen to select something from the treasure box meant I *learned* by watching and modeling good behavior.

All of those roles held something tangible that symbolized achievement. Patrols wore a lime green belt and badge; field day winners took home bright, colorful ribbons, and treasure box recipients could choose from a variety of treats for commendable behavior.

Although I never became a safety patrol officer, I enjoyed several trips to the treasure box the most because it was filled with almost everything a student could imagine – from decorative pencils and scented erasers… to coloring books, trinkets and bubble gum.

Through the years, I've added several precious stones to my personal treasure box of life. I am most proud of my stone of wisdom; it is one of the shiniest because I have had to learn many lessons the hard way. Sometimes the bumps and bruises left from doing things the wrong way remind us to consider a more thought-out approach.

Wisdom taught me that prosperity is more than money, luxurious things, or "arriving"– but it is how we arrive that matters. We must ask ourselves, "How have I poured into others?" "How can I help navigate someone else into their destiny?" True prosperity teaches us the value of sustaining good relationships and being good stewards over possessions and responsibilities. It teaches us to rise to every occasion with our attitude, ego, and character *in check*. It teaches us to master the things that challenge us most or be mastered by those things.

When we surrender to the things that overpower us, we become enslaved to them and we end up serving life sentences in self-imposed prisons. However, the Master's dominant gene of authority dwells within all of us; and *this* gene allows us to be more powerful than we can ever imagine [Luke 10:19]. The key is surrendering our limited power for God's limitless power, which leads us to *His* master plan for our lives.

True prosperity involves humility, balance, love, wisdom, passion, and compassion [I Peter 5:6-8]. It also takes determination and courage to continue running towards life's end zones when the cheerleaders have left the sidelines and your biggest fans, and the band have cleared the stands. Once we've mastered the hardest truth about prosperity, [is it is not about us; no boasting], but to positively influence our corner of the universe, then we will know if we have positioned ourselves to live our fullest life.

Remember when the man wanted to follow Jesus and He told him to sell his belongings, but it saddened him to do so (Matthew 19:16-26). It grieved him because he could not imagine parting with his *possessions*. The sooner we embrace the difficult truth about life not being about just things or having our names in lights, the sooner we *will* discover a solid spiritual foundation compels prosperity and keeps us grounded *when* the benefits of righteous living have manifested. We can best manage our blessings by remaining humble and truly connected to our power source (God) as well as to ourselves and others. In all honesty, we can only reach our highest heights by consistently being lowly positioned... if we constantly practice *going down* in prayer and checking our ego, God will examine our motives and determine when we are prepared for promotion and or increase [Psalm 75:6-7]. God rewards us for diligently seeking Him, not just His hands but His heart.

"Even poverty has a purpose; it can serve as a stepping stone to greatness or a lifetime full of regrets."

~Kandra C. Albury

Poverty is a trap of darkness, *if* it is allowed to be. Fortunately, education empowers each of us with the light of knowledge that leads to freedom and a life-long quest for truth. It opens doors to financial freedom, new ideas and independence. Education allows partakers to multiply and magnify their thinking into tangible opportunities.

Sometimes we create our own limits by applying self-imposed barriers. Obscured vision [or lack thereof] leads to stagnation, fear, intimidation, frustration, and boredom. Vision precedes purpose; consequently, no matter where we find ourselves, it is imperative to write our vision, and speak/pray about our present state so that bountiful blessings can manifest in the very near future.

I recommend writing and praying as if no one is going to read your journal or hear you but God! If you want to be a millionaire—write it, if you want to buy a home or have something you've only dreamed of having, write it! Write until your fingers get tired! We must believe in ourselves and the greatness that resides inside each of us, and I believe it starts by writing and speaking—two powerful forms of communication that *can and will* transform your life.

Too many people struggle with the why, what, when, and what-ifs of life because they have not discovered their God-given DNA, which leads to the discovery of our gifts and the courage to boldly operate in them. I believe that gifts are present when we are children. However, the world teaches us conformity rather than nonconformity. Thus, there are several conformists who settle for what is doable and comfortable… and their lives are consumed by mediocrity. Fortunately, God allows someone to recognize our greatness even when we don't, it could be our parents, a relative, a friend, a neighbor, or teacher… God's sovereignty is the setup of all setups!

When I was in third-grade, my teacher Ms. Bevels had us create an acrostic using our name. The youthful activity taught me a life lesson: there *was and is* more to me than my physical appearance or simply my name. So, regardless of the names I was called, "bald-headed, pickaninny, nappy-headed, black knight, tar baby, and ugly…" I knew there was something great inside of me, and that something great lived in my spirit and manifested in my soul. It was my gusto to not only survive but to live. Today, my namesake is my mantra:

- **K**indhearted
- **A**ttractive
- **N**oble
- **D**istinguished
- **R**esilient
- **A**ppreciative

Kandra means courageous.

"You can be the ugliest person in the world, but if you have a great disposition, people will forget all about how ugly you are."

~ Ms. Emily J. Williams,

Chapter One

It Was All Part of the Master's Plan

With a line filled with annoyed customers, that gave us condescending looks of disdain, momma proudly counted out the food stamps to the grocery store cashier - saying, "These two books got $50, these have $65 each, and this one has all fives, and there's $20 in this one." It was bad enough that we held the line up with our three, overflowing carts of groceries. Momma just had to accurately count and tear the food stamps out of the books for the nonchalant and seemingly *also* annoyed cashier. Momma didn't care about "the people and their faces" [Jeremiah 1:8], because all she could think about was how God had blessed us, yet once again, to have food for the next 30 days. It was humiliating, but I knew we were going to eat good for weeks to come! As long as I had some Debbie Snack Cakes and Moon Pies, I was happy.

Even with five mouths to feed, my mom often shared sandwiches, chips, and drinks with the migrant workers who would knock on our door and ask for something to eat. Sometimes they were dirty, stinky, or even bloody from sporadic fighting.

I was raised on food stamps [throughout my entire childhood]. The food stamps were an unpleasant reminder of *how* poor we really were. However, my hardworking and always-praying mother helped me and my four siblings make the transition from a poverty mindset to a prosperous one; by continually reinforcing that quitting school *wasn't* an option, and believing in God *always* pays off. As for me, I believed that God could do anything, except make us rich!

Back then, Mom was helping us prepare our faith crop for harvesting some 20-years later by planting seeds of hope even though our situation *often* looked and felt hopeless. She went out of her way to teach us the value of working hard, being respectable/respectful, getting good grades, and making good choices.

Although, my mom never said it, her goal was to keep my two brothers out of jail and me and my two sisters from becoming teenage mothers. She would tell us, "I'm going to beat your behind to keep those white folks from beating you because if *they* beat you, they might not know when to stop." Due to my mom's emphatic and seemingly nonstop utterance of the aforementioned words, I grew up fearing white people, striving rigorously to please *them*, while ironically not trusting *them* and feeling purposely bitter towards *them*.

Nonetheless, momma wanted us to beat the odds, and not become a statistic. *This* sometimes meant we had to cut our own switches, getting hit with a shoe, beat with an extension cord, or whatever was closest to her hand. She believed wholeheartedly in that "spare the rod, spoil the child" [No, I am not providing the scripture reference]; I think that was her favorite, ask her. Thus, it wasn't what she put in our milk, but on our butts that kept us out of the juvenile detention center. She stood all of 4 feet and 11 inches, but none of us were deceived by her stature. She could whip all of us at the same time and not miss a beat. However, I sincerely believe she raised us under a tremendous amount of stress and pressure as a single parent.

Momma did what she *could* with what she had. Unsurprisingly, she always made sure we looked polished and "presentable." Momma took my older sister and I to Ms. Grim to get our hair pressed and curled two Saturdays a month. If she couldn't afford it, momma kept a straightening comb in the kitchen to touch up our hair between trips to the beautician.

Ms. Grim also straightened our hair in her kitchen, and mom paid her $5 a head. Ms. Grim was a heavy-set woman with huge breasts, and a high butt. Her jet-black hair was long, and flowed beautifully; she also had a mustache, thus she rarely smiled. What woman would with a full-blown mustache like a man? When straightening the "peas" around my edges, she would put a glob of hair grease on the backside of her hand, rub a dab on my hair, then lean me back on her breast and run the hot comb though my inch- long hair. To get my "kitchen" (the naps in the back of my head) she would lean me forward and get as close as she could to my scalp without burning me. My shoulders would tense up and sometimes I would start sweating. She blew the hot comb as she ran it through my hair, and her breath smelled like turkey hotdogs because she gave mom a few dollars to swing by the corner store to pick up her a pack or two when mom dropped us off. She boiled them on the stove while she straightened my hair.

Ms. Grim hummed spiritual songs as she worked on my hair… I silently and fervently prayed that I did not get burned; that straightening comb was hellishly hot! If it touched my scalp or ear, I felt the burning sensation for days…no matter how much butter she rubbed on the burn to *supposedly* "soothe" it!

Momma said Ms. Grim was gifted at doing hair because while there were other beauticians around town who had graduated cosmetology school and charged more to do the same quality of work, she was self-taught and boy could she make those hot curlers sing!

Ms. Grim was also a deaconess at our church. Momma said she clapped louder than anybody else in the entire church, but that didn't matter to me because she made me look and feel pretty. Besides that, she finished me and my sister's hair before Soul Train came on. When mom picked us up, I hoped and prayed she didn't have to run any additional errands because I wanted to watch Don Cornelius. I always thought he looked like my daddy, and I also wanted to see who I could mimic going down the Soul Train line. We [me and my siblings] danced the entire time the show was on, except when they did the scrabble board. During commercials we took a break from dancing but we knew not to sit on momma's good settee. No one was allowed to sit on the furniture except adults or special company. Momma always exclaimed, "The floor will hold you better than my furniture will!"

Mom drove my brothers one block up the street to Mr. Foreman's Barbershop once or twice a month. However, she never ventured inside and neither did me and my sisters. Even back then, I understood certain things were said and done in a barber shop that girls and women should not be exposed to. There was always a crowd of men waiting to get in "the chair." My brothers were always excited to go to the barbershop—they dashed out of the car like reindeer. That part of town was called "The Corner" and only adults would hang out there and do "adult things." After dropping my brothers off, momma would slowly drive past The Corner in our car that she called a "Studebaker" from time to time.

My mom always had the raggediest, ugliest, and loudest running cars in our neighborhood. In fact, the older I got it seemed like the worse the condition of our cars got. Every time we went out of town, without fail, our car would breakdown.

Mom would get out of the car and flag down a man—any man— to take a look under the hood. Almost every time we needed a jump. After a while she didn't have to flag anyone down because she started doing what she saw others do, which was go to the nearest convenience store, buy a Coca-Cola and pour it on the battery terminals to remove the caked-up acid. Then she'd jump back in the car and fire up the engine. We'd all cheer and mom didn't stop until we arrived home.

One of our cars had to be hot-wired to start, and another had a rusted-out trunk. When we went to the grocery store and on our way home, the canned-goods fell out onto the highway every time momma turned a corner… and true to her shameless nature, momma pulled over and *we* gathered up our monthly blessing. We continued that embarrassing canned-goods chase until she got a piece of paneling and covered the gaping hole in the trunk.

All the kids in our neighborhood picked at our cars, but whenever mom saw them walking, she'd pull over and ask them if they wanted a ride. At first, they appeared a little hesitant, and we *knew* why [heck we were reluctant to ride in it, and it was ours]. Mom drove her cars like she was in the Daytona

500. Even to this day, she calls her 1998 Chevrolet Lumina her "white airplane." She takes pride in taking the elderly people around town to run errands and taking her grandchildren to the park.

I believe growing up poor keeps those [most of us] affected by it humble, grounded, grateful, and kindhearted. Poverty also has a way of fostering the most creative ideas, and my mom was/is undeniably creative. She is the second oldest of six girls, and she was taught early on how to stretch a dollar. A box of baking soda did more than just keep the refrigerator fresh, but it also served as toothpaste and deodorant when momma's money looked funny and her change looked strange.

A lot of kids in our neighborhood received food stamps and free lunch at school, and while several kids at my school complained about how horrible the food was, we had no complaints– none whatsoever. At school, I loved having pancakes and syrup for breakfast, and cheeseburgers and pizzas for lunch. Even today, there are very few things that I *won't* eat or at least try. However, I will not touch liver or beef tripe with a 10-foot pole!

All the kids in our neighborhood joked about receiving food stamps; I saw them as a means to survive. I believe growing up in poverty was a part of God's plan for my life because although we were poor my mom possessed a million-dollar spirit. Yet, as much as I loved my mom, I despised being poor. I grudgingly smiled and faked appreciation for white, knockoff Barbie dolls every Christmas. Although, I liked combing her long, blonde, silky hair, I wanted a doll that looked like me (but without the nappy hair). I wanted us to live like George and Weezy Jefferson from *The Jeffersons*; Heathcliff and Clair Huxtable from *The Cosby Show*, and Vivian and Philip Banks from the *Fresh Prince of Bel-Air*. I also abhorred my family being taunted because of our economic status, but I got used to that. Back then we would poke fun of each other just to pass the time, it was nothing like the bullying children experience today.

From elementary school to high school, once a month, Mom drove 30 minutes to the food stamp office, regardless of the weather, and stood in a line that snaked around the building. We stayed in the car… I watched Momma as she hurried across the street to get in line. After she picked up her food stamps, we headed straight to Jewel T. Mom had a cart, as well as my oldest sister, and my brother had carts too. One of the buggies overflowed with everything like pork chops, ground beef and hotdogs, Vienna sausage, spam, whole chickens, and bacon. The other two carts were filled with canned goods, cereal, soft drinks, and snacks for after-school. She also separated the items that had to be paid for with cash.

Food stamps carried just as much weight as cash. If Mom needed gas and money was low, she'd send us in the corner store one at a time to buy a piece of gum or candy, we brought her the change back and she'd get $5 or $6 worth of gas or some toilet paper—anything that food stamps could or couldn't buy, Mom *still* made them work for us. We did not lack necessities and she made sure of that. Between prayer, the system, and my Mom working different odd jobs, we made it!

An average meal through the week consisted of fried, canned spam, stewed tomatoes with rice, and a tall glass of "red" Kool-Aid. Nothing ever went to waste. Sometimes momma cooked a pot of lima beans and we ate beans, rice and flapjacks for at least three days straight. I always like putting ketchup on my lima beans. Now look at your neighbor and say, "but on Sundays…" we feasted on fried chicken, collard greens, rice, and corn bread. Mom stored our food in the oven and sometimes the roaches would have some of our leftovers, especially the chicken. They would eat holes in it but momma trained us so not to throw out food. So, I cut around the holes where the roaches had helped themselves, and I thanked God for my food, ate, and went to bed.

When I was little, I remember my mom's primary source of income came from cutting ferns. Most days I went to work with her because I wasn't old enough to begin Head Start. I did not like going to work with her because there were snakes and other creepy crawly things that slithered around in the thick, green ferns and they invaded my toys.

One day, as Mom cut the ferns I heard this deafening scream. A snake had wrapped itself around her boot. She made quite a scene trying to get away from that snake!

Mom cut approximately 200-300 bunches a day at 27¢ a bunch. Each bunch contained 20 pieces of fern that she wrapped in a rubber band and stacked them in a pile. The truck load of ferns was shipped to florists across the country.

I enjoyed one thing about going to work with Mom, and that was playing with Mr. Causey's daughters, Spring and

Sandra. The Causey's were good people and they owned several ferneries. The Causey girls were very pretty. Both of them had long, beautiful blonde hair, rosy lips, and pretty eyes. They lived in a tall, gray and white house near the fern fields. They also had four wheelers and every so often they took me for a spin through the fern patch. It was the most exciting thing ever!

Today, the migrant workers have taken over the fern cutting industry in Crescent City, and Mr. Causey passed away in 2012. Before he passed, Mom said she'd run into him in the store and they shared long reminiscent conversations about the 'good old days.' I don't know what was so good about cutting ferns all year round in all kinds of weather.

Mom worked several years cutting ferns to provide for us. She recalled, one day cutting ferns and the next day she gave birth to my brother Cory [what maternity leave?]. She cut fern until her back gave out from staying bent over - six to eight hours a day. For this reason, Momma ended up going back to school when I was in middle school. Even now, she mentions severe back pain and I know exactly what caused it– her relentless love and determination to keep a meal on the table, clothes on our backs, and a roof over our heads.

To transition from the hard labor of cutting ferns, Mom started keeping the migrant workers' children while *they* cut ferns. She became the first entrepreneur in my family when she opened a home daycare. I arrived home from school and there would be ten or more babies all over our three-bedroom-one-bathroom home. Two or three babies were in the playpen, two more were in walkers, three of them sometimes napped on the couch, and two of them happily swung in baby-swings. Back then, home daycare providers didn't have to be licensed. Mom had a handwritten sign on the front door reflecting the amount she charged, hours of operation and a special note emphasizing the time all children had to be picked up. She even tried to speak Spanish to communicate with parents, and when they couldn't understand her or vice versa, she would ask someone who was bilingual to translate for her.

Many of my childhood memories were good, but I also remember how being deprived caused a lot of my own personal stress and anxiety. In elementary school, I had to wear

Rustler Jeans, which were for boys because if they were on sale at Pic N' Save that's what momma bought. I prayed each day that I wore them (about three days a week) that no one realized that I was wearing boy jeans. I'd pull my shirt as far is it could go to conceal the Rustler name on the pockets. To make matters worse, my godfather cut off all my hair because the chemicals from boxed relaxers had taken my hair out in patches, which is why Momma started taking me to Ms. Grim; Mom said she had "growing hands."

Strangely enough, my brother Cory had the biggest afro ever. His hair was so long that Mom groomed his hair in pigtails and he cried because he knew the kids in our neighborhood and at school would call him a girl. He was right, too, because the kids teased him... and most adults mistakenly thought he was a girl and thought I was a boy, and oh how I despised that!

I started working summer jobs when I was twelve years old. I worked cleaning the local elementary school that I attended from kindergarten to fifth-grade. I scrubbed the tops of desks, scraped bubblegum from under desks; removed gum from carpets, and polished blackboards. However, by the time

I turned 15, I had gotten a real part-time job at Miller's, the town's only grocery store. I worked there as a bagger and cashier to take some of the load off my mom, who at that time had gone back to school and earned two certifications– one was a Child Development Associate certification (CDA) to work in daycares and the other, a Certified Nursing Assistant certification (CNA) to work in healthcare. Several of my classmates also worked at the city's only local grocery store. When my mom came in the store, I got off my register and went to the bathroom or walked to the back of the store while she paid for our groceries with food stamps. I was *still* embarrassed.

I made a pact with myself to never use food stamps or if I had to use them, it wouldn't be for a long period of time. Either way, it was shameful for my classmates to know that we received food stamps. Funny thing is quite a few people knew (or at least I thought they did) but they never mentioned it to me.

During my sophomore year of high school, I tried out for the cheerleading squad. I didn't know much about cheering, but I knew I wanted to wear one of those cute uniforms.

Not to mention, I *knew* I had what was needed to be a cheerleader (a loud mouth, fairly decent grades, and a sparkling personality). Anxiously, I tried out and made the JV squad and cheered my sophomore, junior, and senior year.

I thought it was paradoxical that I accomplished so much while being raised in poverty. After all, why would anyone with so little have anything to cheer about? I paid for my own uniform, cheer camps, and food after the games.

I was second runner up on the homecoming court while on food stamps and was voted the most-spirited! I served on senior counsel and worked hard in Future Business Leaders of America (FBLA) and Girls Action or (GA) with my high school journalism teacher, Mrs. Gail Williams.

We went to church every Sunday and prayed to God for "a way out..." at least *I* did. I wanted to catch that same *morning train* that the saints sung about, straight out of poverty! My mom would told us to look like we had $100 in our pocket even if you only had a $1, and I hated faking it! I wanted to live in a large house, have my own room, not get my sister's hand-me-downs, and not have to wear clothes from Pic 'N Save. I didn't want any parts of being poor, but I had to persevere through that process—it wasn't like I had a say in the family God bestowed unto me *as a blessing.*

My mom was a parent in the context of a noun as well as a verb. To parent is to be there in action, correcting, loving, teaching, leading, sacrificing and guiding–that was my mom! My mom never played when it came to rearing us. She worked jobs that allowed her to be home by the time we got out of school.

When my mom worked as a CNA at a local nursing home, the floor supervisor came to her as she was finishing her 7:30 a.m. – 4:30 p.m. shift and asked if she could pull a double. My mom's response:

"I haven't finished this single and when I do, I'm going to get my pocketbook, jump on the elevator and go home to tend to my children!" I still laugh when she tells me this story.

My mom is my BFF but it wasn't until I was grown and could help her pay some of her bills that my mom became my best friend. She always told us that since she had to raise us by herself we had to do what she said; no ifs, ands, or buts about it! Dignity, respect and getting our lesson were non-negotiable as far as Mom was concerned.

Wherever we showed out, that's where she corrected us. Her favorite parental chant was, "I have to cut your behind where you show out because something may happen to me between the time you act up and the time I get you home!"

We were chastised ["got a whooping"] for five things: lying, stealing, talking back to adults, breaking things around the house, and bringing home bad grades. She also whipped us if my siblings and I fought each other or if we misbehaved in church or school. I remember my brother talking back while mom cooked dinner one evening. She casually walked away from the stove, entered the living room, hit him in the nose, and went back to frying chicken. He buckled over nursing his nose; I simply looked and remained quiet, I wasn't going to say anything!

The greatest thing my mom did was take us to church, and she continued her insistence during our teen years. While at church I understood more about God and then invited Him into my heart to be my God. Sunday mornings were the best, because the weekends were the only time that we were awakened to the smell of bacon, eggs, grits or pancakes. On the Lord's Day, Momma's terminology for Sundays, she blasted her James Cleveland eight-track. I remember the song vividly: *"Jesus is the best thing that ever happened to me."*

My mom didn't take any wooden nickels from anyone, particularly my dad; who she constantly harassed about taking better care of us.

My dad was a strange man. His mother lived next door to us so he drove past our home to get to my grandmother's house. Sometimes he stopped and I hopped on the back of his truck for the short drive to my Grandma Vator's house. I always asked him for money and he gave me the same tired response, "Baby, Daddy ain't got no money."

I didn't understand his lack of money because he owned the most popular juke joint in Putnam County called *Dream Land*. It was also called *Vernal's* after my grandfather, but my mom called it the Devil's den. He and my Auntie Ruth ran the juke joint and he made a lot of money, whether he admits it or not. People traveled near and far to dance to the jukebox, buy hot fish and chicken sandwiches, gamble in the front door, and drink.

One thing Daddy did not tolerate was fighting, he didn't want 'the law' called to his place. His nickname was Cap, and I heard he earned that name because he packed heat, and was never afraid to use it.

Sometimes Momma piled me and my siblings into Bessie, the sputtering, green 1970 Malibu, to do late night drive-bys to gauge the crowd at the juke joint. She wanted to make sure Daddy was still in business and could pay his child support. We saw cars parked alongside the road miles before getting there. Momma slowed down as we neared the front of the building then punched the gas. She repeated her stakeout routine until she was satisfied. If we were sitting up, the sudden acceleration threw us back in the seat!

My dad never drank or smoked so addictions didn't keep him from his financial obligations, but I heard he loved going to play the dogs.

I remember one weekend Momma let us spend a Saturday with him. She must have been stressed or something because she never let us go anywhere with Daddy. I was so excited because I had waited [seemingly all my life], for the day I could spend quality time with Daddy. He picked us up and we went straight to the juke joint. He cleaned and stocked the beer and liquor, while me and my older sister

tried to contain our excitement over this forbidden adventure. I couldn't believe I was actually inside that place! If Momma knew we were inside 'Devil's Den,' she would have fainted.

'Nature called' while we were there, but the bathroom was filthy, so I held it… and then I discovered the juke box. The door where all of the change fell was open. I had never seen so many quarters! I yelled, "Hey Daddy, can I have some quarters?" He annoyingly shouted, "No, I have to pay the people for the machine!" I thought to myself, "Momma's right, Daddy's just plain old stingy." I was ready to go home.

When he dropped us off I felt sadly disappointed. He didn't buy any ice cream cones; there were no walks in the park, no fishing, no nothing! I wondered if his daddy was a grouch and ignored him, like he did us. Whatever the reason for his distant behavior, he drew a distorted picture of what a father should be, and Momma didn't make it any better because she intentionally exposed his shortcomings every opportunity she had. When he passed our house, Momma yelled out the door, "I'm going to see what the white man has to say about you not paying child support for these children!"

I'd heard that the child support judge, Mr. Eastmoore, told those who didn't pay their child support to bring their toothbrush with them the next time they appeared in front of him, meaning their consequent destination was the gray bar hotel.

Nonetheless, Momma made up in her mind that *her* children would be respectful, smart, and productive Christian citizens. She often said, "I want more than just me to love you, I want other people to love you too." Funny thing is she'd say that right before she whipped us.

My momma was a lady. Before she ventured *anywhere*, she ordered my siblings and I to help put on her girdle… our fingertips burned something awful from all of the tugging and pulling. My brothers attempted to hide every time momma called us to help pull up her corset; but she needed all hands-on deck for that undertaking. She also wore a slip under her dresses. She believed that ladies should be modest in dress and in their actions. She wasn't big on makeup, but God knows she wore a lot of rouge on her cheeks and she kept that red face sponge handy to keep the shine off her face, she even used it to wipe our faces, my brothers hated. After getting dressed, she sprayed herself down with Charlie perfume. This was Momma's regimen whether she traveled into town or church.

We were in church *almost* every time the doors opened; I believe momma kept us in church to keep us out of trouble. She ensured that we sat on the pew in front of her, so when we misbehaved she could easily tap us on the shoulder and give us *the eye*. If we *really* 'acted up,' Momma popped us on the back of our heads. Truth be told, I didn't mind sitting close to the front of the church because that meant I could see all the action, especially during praise and worship. Most times it felt like Show Time at the Apollo.

During testimony service people sang their songs and boasted about the goodness of the Lord [whether it was how a bill got paid or how the Lord had healed them]. Praise and worship was the time that the people would just let it "all hang out," in Jesus' name of course. The adults urged the children to stand up and share something that God had done for *them* as well.

If there were parishioners that didn't have the opportunity to testify, everyone stood and testified in unison or "under one voice". I thought it was rude and annoying, especially since we were taught to wait our turn to speak! There was always *that* one person left standing who went on and on about the Lord, causing the drummer to "tune-up" and get the saints happy all over again!

Church seemed chaotic but ironically entertaining to me. Going to church was like going to a pep rally. People brought in rub boards; wooden blocks; three to four spoons bound together with a rubber band, and of course the staple instrument found in all Pentecostal churches —the tambourine. It was played by the young and the old. Many of the tambourines only had three or four cymbals intact after being played at every church service. The saints made so much noise during praise and worship; they could've raised the dead!

We knew *not* to laugh in church while the Holy Ghost *had its way!* Momma didn't play that! However, when my siblings and I got home, we hosted our own comedy show as mocked how the saints' wigs and glasses flew off, and how some of them danced right out of their shoes. We even imitated how some people just fainted, causing the ushers to storm in with sheets, fans, and glasses of water.

After all that "churching," and enduring the pastor's two-hour fire and brimstone sermon, there was a smorgasbord of fried chicken, macaroni and cheese, potato salad, perlo rice, cakes galore, and Kool-Aid in the kitchen. The pastor and his family always ate first and everyone else followed suit. Not only did the pastor and his family eat first, he always drove a big, fancy car while most of the members' cars sputtered, skipped and popped to and from church... *well, ours did.*

No matter how much everyone else may have gotten caught up in the Holy Ghost "hype," Mom remained focused and put what was most important first... God, then us! In fact, Mom even let us dress up and go trick-or-treating when the pastor called it the Devil's holiday. Although, she was one of the first to holler amen when the pastor bashed Halloween; she allowed us go trick-or-treating with our friends. Mom went against the grain for us.

Mom never wore big fancy hats or expensive suits; she didn't pay every assessment or give an offering every time we went to church either. She stayed within her means and lived a grounded *yet* balanced life. I remember asking her why she didn't wear big hats like all the other ladies and she said, "Fancy hats are good and all but you sure can't eat them." I believe she meant it was a waste of her money to buy a hat when bills had to be paid. She seldom bought herself anything new, but made sure we had, particularly at Easter and Christmas. For our birthdays, she never ordered cakes from Publix, but baked one fresh in our kitchen and she decorated them with edible kits.

She seldom took us to the doctor and used all sorts of over-the-counter medications such as Father John's, 666 cough syrup, castor oil, Vicks Vapor Rub, and the worst of them all… Black Draught. She lined all of us up on Fridays for a tablespoon full of that yucky stuff that sent all of us running to the bathroom at once. It was horrid, especially since we only had one bathroom!

Mom wasn't too bad with her home remedies as others were... I heard that my Grandma Rosa gave my cousins kerosene with sugar, gin, honey, lemon, and turpentine to get rid of their colds. I'm simply glad everyone lived to talk about the so-called "home" remedies.

The adages detailed below are things I heard constantly from Momma as a child, and even today. The most important thing is, these sayings have kept me grounded through the years. I wholeheartedly believe there's nothing like good old-fashioned manners and southern raising:

- Treat people the way you want to be treated because you never know who you're going to need.

- It's not what you say but how you say it.

- If you mess up, cleanup... we don't have a maid service.

- God sits high and looks low beholding the good and the evil.

- You can fool some of the people some of the time, but you can't fool God none of the time.

- Do not mess with quiet people because they'll hurt you.

- Don't leave one job until you have another one.

- It's better to give than to receive.

- I whip you because I love you! This behind cutting is going to hurt me more than it will hurt you!

- Fix yourself up when you go out because you never know who you're going to meet.

- Do your work right the first time and you won't have to do it again.

- Those teachers have their education, now you have to get yours.

- Speak to people when you see them; even a dog says good morning by wagging its tail.

- People don't want to be around you if you act ugly. They'll hate to see you coming and be glad to see you go!

- When you get an education in your head, no one can take it from you.

- Watch how you treat me because you will need me before I need you.

- Don't let your mouth write a check that your behind can't cash!

- Don't look in grown people's mouths when they are talking!

- What you put in is what you get out–nothing more, nothing less!

- If you eat too much candy, your teeth will rot right out of your head!

- Don't keep coming in and out—either stay in or stay out!

- What won't kill you will surely make you stronger.

- Boys tell every girl she's cute.

- Answer grown people yes ma'am and yes sir. Respect will take your further than money.

- Answer me when I'm talking to you.

- Even if you don't have but a dollar in your pocket act like you have a million!

- Tell God thank you for your food because somebody somewhere doesn't have food to eat.

- Say thank you because people don't have to do anything.

- Don't let dark catch you outside.

- Go cut me a switch. (I'd always bring back a twig)

- If you lie, you'll steal, and if you steal you'll kill!

- Birds of a feather flock together!

- Don't follow the crowd, because the crowd isn't always right!

- Roll your eyes at me again and they'll be rolling on the floor!

- You can draw bees better with honey than you can with vinegar!

- Sit up straight- don't slouch!

- Stop dragging your feet when you walk, you sound lazy!

"But God hath chosen the foolish things of the world to confound the wise; and God hath chosen the weak things of the world to confound the things which are mighty;"

~I Corinthians 1:27

Chapter Two

Early Exposure Equals Life Composure

My childhood has served as a reminder that nothing is impossible. I have always felt that God had a plan for my life. Even when I ended up on the cheerleading squad, I knew God was up to something. Back then, there weren't many cheerleaders who looked like me, but that didn't bother me because all I wanted to do was cheer, scream, and be free, even though I knew very little about football or basketball.

As a cheerleader, I often had the opportunity to practice at my teammates' houses. Some of their houses were nestled on lakes, and their parents were teachers and business executives. I saw my teammates' fathers come in from work with their briefcases and kiss their wives. I walked into their homes and felt as if I had entered a palace; their houses had high ceilings, catwalks, kitchens with islands, pots dangling over my head, and offices with computers. They also had pools. I thought to myself, "Mom is right about education leading to success." These folks had education, worked *good* jobs, drove nice cars, and lived in nice neighborhoods. I yearned for the same thing, especially a family with both parents for my children.

My teammates taught me *almost* everything… from how to shave, to how to properly cut a steak. They embodied the American Dream, and I decided during my adolescent years that nothing would stop me from getting *my* piece of the pie. Poverty, lack, or anything associated with *these* words would take residence in my future.

Now one thing I knew *not* to do, that they got away with… was telling their parents to shut up and slamming doors! Let's just say I wanted to keep my teeth in my mouth and my head on my shoulders.

When I was in high school I was a member of Girls Action or GA. We served the community and conducted outreach events quite frequently. One of our field trips included visiting various churches. It was during a field trip to a Catholic church that I learned to appreciate how others worshiped God.

Nonetheless, being exposed to different people and religions early on inspired me to believe that I was supposed to make a comfortable living, I was destined to be successful, I was created to dream out loud, and I was positioned to have access to things if I worked hard. I was supposed to eat steak, live in a nice neighborhood, and drive a car with air conditioning (that didn't cut off at every stop sign or red light). It was perfectly OKAY to accept people who looked, acted, and worshipped God differently than I did. The key to acceptance is early exposure to various cultures, religions, lifestyles and beliefs.

I had never stepped foot on a college campus until I attended a cheerleading camp the summer of 1990, at the University of Florida. Simply seeing the students as they biked around campus or walked to class inspired me. While we rode across campus to our dorm, I noticed that the red, brick buildings were unusually tall. As a resident of Crescent City, a town with one traffic light and fewer than 2,000 residents; I felt as if I had seen the world... my world for the first time!

The University of Florida was a place of honor, academic excellence, and excitement. I told myself, "I will attend "this" school, and I did 12 years later to pursue a master's degree in mass communications!

Make a personal pact with yourself, remember it, write it down, and recite it [out loud]. Remind yourself that you *are* great and *can* achieve greatness. Remind yourself about what it takes to achieve greatness and how you can share your greatness with others. When you expose yourself to new people, places, and things you obtain something valuable from the experience, and you add value to yourself as well as others.

"Though it tarries, wait for it."

Habakkuk 2:2

In my early 20's and 30's, I often rode through the "Beverly Hills" sides of town to admire the homes and cars parked in the driveways; I refer to it as, "vision building." I'm certain the residents perceived my "vision building" as suspicious, but I needed to envision what was/and became possible for me.

Walt Disney once said, "It is kind of fun to do the impossible." Today his legacy lives on because his theme parks attract millions of tourists from around the world to experience the magic of Disney.

We must believe what may be impossible to some can be made possible through us! I believe each of us has the aptitude to make the impossible possible.

When we are on a mission in life, we must become our first investor of hope, faith, vision, ambition and fortitude. When I was in 10th grade, I told my high school guidance counselor that I wanted to go to college to become a journalist. I had been writing for my school's newspaper for two years and enjoyed it. She told me that I didn't have what it took to succeed in college and my best option would be to attend a vocational school and "take up" a trade. *I knew she was lying!*

I had a problem with her counsel as it contradicted everything that my mother and grandmother had always told me, which was, "Don't let anyone tell you what you cannot do because you can do anything if you put your mind to it."

I left her office angry and utterly bewildered, because what she claimed opposed what had been instilled in me since I was a little girl. I shared the occurrence with my mom when I got home. She was at the kitchen sink preparing dinner. As I explained what happened she never looked at me. Once I said, the guidance counselor told me that I wasn't good enough for college my mom looked over her shoulder and said to me, "Remember what I taught you." I smiled and knew that I was going to make Ms. Guidance Counselor out of a liar, and I did just that!

By the time I graduated high school, I had received five scholarships to attend college. I started at the community college, then transferred to the University of North Florida, then the University of Florida, and finally Truth Bible University.

My progression was intentional and unstoppable. However, I had my share of pit stops… including a failed relationship from my first marriage. The marriage lasted eight years; truthfully, the relationship was toxic before we vowed "I do."

When my ex-husband and I were dating, I told him that I wanted to end the relationship a couple of times but could never seem to break it off. One day we went to the mall so that he could "question" a friend of mine [while she was 'on the clock'] about my "relationship" with someone else. When he didn't hear the response that he suspected, he grabbed me by the hand and rushed out the store.

On our way out of the mall, he grabbed me around the neck and threw me against the chains of a store that had gone out of business. I picked myself up from the floor and knew if I followed him to the car, something terrible was going to happen. Back then people didn't walk around with camera phones, but I kind of wished they did because I was too afraid to scream for help. My car was parked behind the mall.

Once we got in the car, we exchanged words then out of nowhere... a blow to the left side of my face. It was so hard that everything around me seemed to spin. I shook my head hoping it would stop; before I could react, he jumped on top of me, locked the door and started punching. All I could do was attempt to scratch his eyes out and cover my face. I wet my pants trying to fight him off...I guess you could say he beat the pee out of me.

When I was finally able to unlock the door, I ran to a man nearby and screamed for help; he told me he would not get involved. My ex-husband threw my purse out of the window and fled the scene. I hid at my friends' houses for a couple of days. When those outside of my trusted circle asked what happened, I told them that I ran into a box in the storage room at my job where I worked as a cashier. *That* lie haunted me throughout my marriage.

Shortly after that incident, I learned that I was pregnant with first my daughter Drea. In an attempt to keep folk from talking bad about me, I got married at 19 and had her at 20. We were two broken and incomplete people who became a married and incomplete mess.

I remained in the abusive marriage while completing my studies at St. Johns River State College. I even worked at a furniture factory to pay for my classes one semester. It was hard work and it was hot! From the time I clocked in until the end of the shift, furniture came in on an assembly line. I chased furniture the entire time, and I was responsible for wiping off the excess furniture polish to help ensure an even finish. My hands and clothes were filthy, but I needed the money to pay for my last two courses so that I could graduate. After I received my check (two weeks later), I never returned to the "hot box" factory!

I eventually got the courage to file for divorce following another violent incident. I was left picking up the pieces and struggling to learn who I was, find healing, and adjust to maintaining a household as a single mom, but according to God's plan, I was still on track.

Thanks to the Tom Joyner Morning Show (TJMS) Christmas Wish, they helped me bring my student loans current so that I could start at UF in the fall of 2001. So many things transpired during that year. I had lost my beloved Grandma Rosa in April, my divorce was final in June and I planned on starting my studies in August.

I recall feeling tremendously overwhelmed prior to starting my studies. However, I understood that there are times when we just have to choose to believe… even when the odds are stacked against us—even if what we are trying to accomplish is something that has never been done before—is it imperative to *still* believe! When we choose to believe in the "happily ever after factor," which is seeing the end without focusing too much on the journey itself, it gives us that much more energy to master our situation. I am not saying to ignore the trials during the journey, but don't become consumed by the challenges involved the process.

I believed that what I saw and said at the cheerleading camp during the summer of 1990 positioned me to accomplish my dream of attending UF in 2001. In addition, I worked hard to achieve my goals in high school, junior college, and at the University of North Florida. Regardless of the difficulties and disappointments I faced, God knew my heart's desires and granted them.

During the admissions process to UF, I decided to move back home after my divorce. My mom helped me raise the girls and I continued working at the *Palatka Daily News* as a general assignment reporter. Because my car had been totaled in a car accident, I didn't have a car or a job in the area where I had moved. Also, my student loan was in default but I kept on working, saving, praying, and anticipating a move to Gainesville to start college.

I originally wrote the Tom Joyner Morning Show (TJMS) asking for a new set of tires for my car that ended up a total loss. So when the station's representative called and asked for information about the tires, I told her about the accident. The woman on the other end of the phone said, "Well, I guess you don't need us," but I stopped her in the middle of what she was saying and explained how I needed my student loans out of default status so that I could begin my studies in the fall. She asked me the amount and captured some additional information; she also asked me to write a letter and submit it to her via fax. A couple of days later, as I test drove a new car my cell phone rang. It was the lady that I had spoken with earlier in the week from TJMS. She said Tom approved your Christmas Wish and my letter would be read on the air during the show. She said a check would be mailed directly to the school's financial aid office. I was blown away! In a matter of five days I got another car (the one that I test drove), an apartment, a job in the city, and my student loan was no longer in default status.

I did not allow myself to be distracted or overwhelmed, but I shifted my focus, prayed faithfully, and worked my disadvantage to my advantage.

"When Peter stepped off the boat he became distracted and began to sink. Don't become too districted while on your assignment."

Matthew 14: 28-31

Chapter Three

When Your Pit Stops Prepare You for Your Purpose

Sometimes you have to pull into the pit stop to refuel and get back in the race.

As a child, it wasn't uncommon for me to see the drivers competing in the Daytona 500 come through town with their race cars hitched to their fancy motor coaches. My brothers could recognize the cars and the drivers a mile away. Dale Earnhardt, Sr. and Richard Petty were their favorites. We watched the races on TV after church on Sunday. I never cared much for watching the actual race because I was always fascinated by the pit crews.

Drivers drove into the pit for fuel, tire changes, and quick checks under the hood. It was the job of the pit crew to get the driver back on the track as fast as possible. They knew how to top off the gas, change the oil and all four tires simultaneously. Everyone had a job and they knew exactly what it was, and how to do it efficiently and effectively to get the driver out of the pit and back on the track in record time.

I utilized this analogy because there are times in life that we will find ourselves in the pit stop. I encourage everyone to see their pit stop as a place to strategize, regroup, refuel, set goals and be productive. I've had to pull into the pit stop for my third, fourth, and fifth wind. I had to ensure my pit crew (friends) were equipped to help me get back into the race.

It is vital to have the *right* crew members in the pit because the last thing you need is someone putting down nails or putting sugar in your gas tank while you're trying to get back in the race.

Now the question is, how can we be productive while in the pit? I recommend setting new goals, reevaluating old ones, and remaining in motion. Find enough courage to outweigh the fear, and attain a child-like perspective…in the eyes of a child, nothing is impossible. Remember, we are all born with the will to survive; we just must tap into it during our pitstop experiences.

"Don't allow life's pitstops to become

a final destination."

~Kandra C. Albury

WE HAVE THE DNA TO SURVIVE AND BE TRIUMPHANT

When I think about how we are all born with survival instincts, I think about the Baby Jessica story. The 18-month-old girl fell into a well in a backyard in Texas. I think everyone around the world wanted the little girl to hold onto life until rescuers reached her. We prayed and hoped for the best. Jessica spent more than 48 hours in a dark, cold well. Food and water were passed down to her, and amazingly enough she survived.

Considering the servicemen and women who protect/defend our freedom to miners trapped 4.5 miles under the earth's surface…God granted everyone supernatural survival instincts and it is engrained within our DNA.

When I worked for an academic medical center, my job duties included writing patient stories and coordinating video shoots. A common thread of each patient's story was their will to survive. Their desire to beat the odds and give death a run for its money set the stage for the miraculous to happen. It often seemed at the point when many of them were faced with a life-threatening injury or a disease their need to survive outweighed their will to give up.

I had the privilege of meeting several patients, their spouses, and other close family members in their homes. Almost all of them said they relied on their survival instincts and prayer to guide them through their situations. Three of my most memorable stories include the story of a four-year-old little girl who plummeted 15 feet from a second-story bedroom window and landed in the driveway; a mother of three who was diagnosed with an aggressive form of breast cancer, and a pastor who waited six years for a kidney transplant.

Survival Story #1

It was President's Day 2009, when a beautiful blue-eyed, four-year-old girl went upstairs to get her blanket to return downstairs to watch TV with her parents. However, she was distracted by her sisters who were playing outside. Her mom had left the window open after doing some spring cleaning. The little girl leaned against the screen to talk to her two older sisters and the screen instantly gave into the gravity of the pressure… she plummeted 15 feet and onto the driveway.

Her mom said during the ambulance ride, she sat on the floor next to her daughter hoping to keep her alert. She stared into her daughter's eyes but she didn't say a word. Her mother kept talking and repeating herself then the little girl squeezed her hand. It was then that both she and her daughter tapped into hope and the will to survive.

She said after her daughter squeezed her hand she knew everything would be OK... even if the road to recovery seemed endless. Doctors said falls of this nature could cause abnormal functioning such as sleepiness, seizures and vomiting. After receive ng around-the-clock care for five days, the little girl was discharged. Her family said their faith and support from their friends got them through that difficult time. The little girl started kindergarten August 2011. She survived and beat the odds.

Survival Story #2

When a married mother of three discovered a lump in her breast, in early 2009, she said she knew it was the unthinkable. The year prior, her younger sister who was in her late 20's was diagnosed with the same disease. They both tested positive for the breast cancer gene. She said she only allowed herself a five minute breakdown on her drive home while her doctors charted a treatment plan. She opted to have both breasts removed, underwent breast reconstructive surgery, and endured chemotherapy treatments. Her biggest fear was losing her hair, but she took that very well and in a span of seven months went from a diagnosis and treatment to recovery, which ended with what she called a "boob job."

Survival Story #3

When we meet most pastors, it's seldom that we expect them to be challenged in their faith. However, this pastor who was a healthy, third-degree black belt found himself having to exercise the same faith he preached from his pulpit, within his life.

In mid-2004, he went to see his primary care physician and the doctor informed him that there was a problem with his kidneys. His doctor ordered lab tests, and they indicated abnormal creatinine levels in his blood. Creatinine is a by-product of normal muscle contractions and is removed from the blood through the kidneys. When the kidneys malfunction for any reason, creatinine levels increase in the blood. High levels of creatinine threaten kidney failure. The two most common causes of kidney failure are high blood pressure and diabetes. In the pastor's case, it was high blood pressure. His wife of 35 years said they both were in complete shock because she said they had always followed through with their healthcare providers.

While going to dialysis three days a week, three hours a day, the 72-year-old pastor preached on Sundays and taught Bible study on Wednesday nights. He also spent time fishing and working on the church's newsletter via his computer (impressive to say the least).

Then on March 9, 2010, his wait for a kidney was over. He received the organ and his body didn't reject it. He's been healthy since his transplant and continues to pastor.

He said even while going to dialysis he spent much of his time encouraging other patients. He said staying focused on his earthly mission built his faith and helped him endure the six-year wait.

The pastor remained occupied, even in his pit, just as Luke 19:13 reads:

> *"Before he left, he called together ten of his servants and divided among them ten pounds of silver, saying, 'Invest this for me while I am gone.'"*

Here, the King James Version actually says to occupy: *"And he called his ten servants, and delivered them ten pounds, and said unto them,* **Occupy** *till I come."*

Never say never—for real

There were several things that I said I would never do; one was become a school teacher, have children and get married again after my divorce (although I knew God created me to be a wife). I also said I didn't want any part of food stamps because I always felt embarrassed to spend them.

However, everything I said I would never do… I have done them, all through the grace of God and I was OK. I once read that God uses our plans as the punch line *for* his jokes. Well… I must be heaven's laughingstock.

I received food stamps for a short period of time as a single mother. Grocery shopping was slightly less embarrassing because I didn't have books of food stamps but an EBT card, which provided some privacy. I also utilized subsidized medical insurance for the girls (Florida Kidcare). I went for long periods of time without health insurance, but I knew if something happened to me, I could find something in my medicine cabinet or at the local pharmacy that would provide some relief. My Momma also prayed the sick away after she showed up with her medicine grip, and pumped me full of soup and home remedies.

I sealed my health with a prayer of faith that nothing serious would happen to me. Out of the four years that I lived in Gainesville, I caught the flu two years in a row, and like I said, my Momma took good care of me. Thank heaven for Thera Flu, orange juice, Vick's Vapor Rub and lots of chicken noodle soup.

Chapter Four
Mentality Shift Equals Lifestyle Shift

"No temptation has overtaken you except what is common to mankind. AND GOD IS FAITHFUL; he will not let you be tempted beyond what you can bear. But when you are tempted, he will also provide a way out so that you can endure it." 1 Corinthians 10:13, NIV

Transitioning from a food stamp mentality to a favor mentality isn't easy, especially when you are deemed ineligible to receive assistance. It is at this point the decision must be made… either survive without assistance or remain in a cycle of poverty. Some, contently linger in poverty because it's convenient, comfortable, and familiar. Getting out of poverty will challenges one's character; builds endurance, and incites determination.

Recipients decide telling the truth regarding their income or the number of individuals in their household, is far more valuable than the *'benefits of poverty.'* When truth is compromised, it sets the stage for a life-style of lack, generational poverty, and closed doors. God does not honor lying or cheating but he honors truth and integrity.

I chose to survive and I had already positioned myself to endure because I had started investing in my education–even if I had thousands of dollars in student loans. The five scholarships I received for community college paved the way for expanding my academic career. My mom also sowed seeds of hope into my academic future, but I had to work my fields of aspiration to expect an abundant harvest.

I made several pitstops on the way to my success end zones. Consequently, I understood, how imperative it was to keep a forward-focused mindset; I realized the purpose in the pit stops! I knew that I couldn't afford to forfeit my scholarships, my children were depending on me, and I wasn't going to let them or myself down. My Mom beamed with pride when I shared my future plans with her. Her smile gave me the will to see beyond my situations. Simply picturing the happiness on her face fueled my passion to leave an indelible mark on my Momma's heart.

One of my most memorable jobs while in graduate school was as a part-time teacher at PACE Center for Girls. It paid $18 an hour at 25 hours a week. I was thankful, but it wasn't enough. The three-room school house offered a number of support services to its students. Many of the services helped me become more aware, accountable, loveable, and teachable. I learned to celebrate my uniqueness as a woman. The girls taught me to wear my tenacity like a badge of honor. They gave me hope and inspired me to be a better mom to my own daughters. I believe God had me there for a reason. I always said I would never teach, but the longer I stayed the easier it was for me to give into God's purpose, which was to love, share, teach, and remain teachable.

Even when our vision is obscured in unfavorable situations, being the hope of someone else's resilience has a way of compelling our will to keep going. Those girls were my driving force; they helped me see my way through when I thought there was no way. Hugging them when I needed a hug filled a void in my life and vice versa. When I didn't know if or how things were going to work out in my personal life; their well-being and academic success served as a much-needed distraction for me.

Here's what some of my students had to say about me:

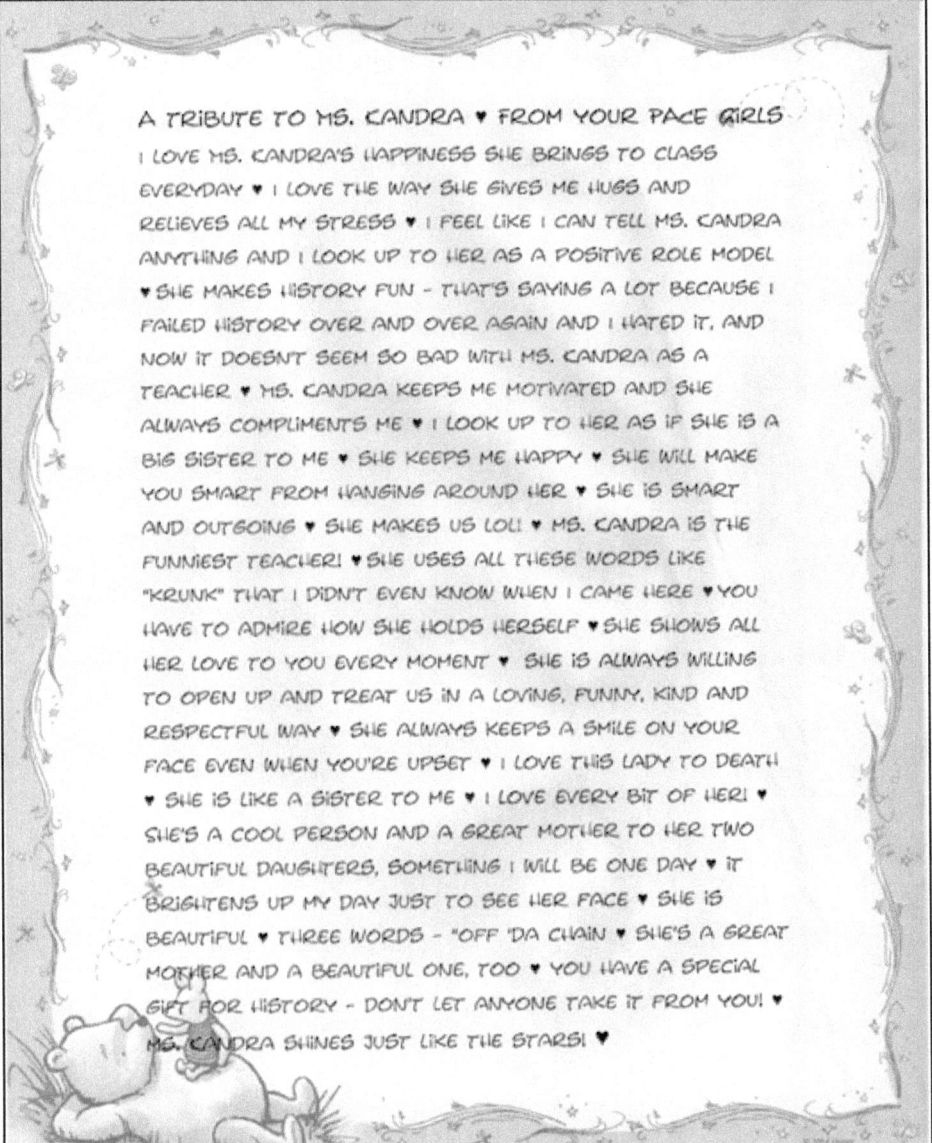

A TRIBUTE TO MS. KANDRA ♥ FROM YOUR PACE GIRLS
I LOVE MS. KANDRA'S HAPPINESS SHE BRINGS TO CLASS EVERYDAY ♥ I LOVE THE WAY SHE GIVES ME HUGS AND RELIEVES ALL MY STRESS ♥ I FEEL LIKE I CAN TELL MS. KANDRA ANYTHING AND I LOOK UP TO HER AS A POSITIVE ROLE MODEL ♥ SHE MAKES HISTORY FUN – THAT'S SAYING A LOT BECAUSE I FAILED HISTORY OVER AND OVER AGAIN AND I HATED IT, AND NOW IT DOESN'T SEEM SO BAD WITH MS. KANDRA AS A TEACHER ♥ MS. KANDRA KEEPS ME MOTIVATED AND SHE ALWAYS COMPLIMENTS ME ♥ I LOOK UP TO HER AS IF SHE IS A BIG SISTER TO ME ♥ SHE KEEPS ME HAPPY ♥ SHE WILL MAKE YOU SMART FROM HANGING AROUND HER ♥ SHE IS SMART AND OUTGOING ♥ SHE MAKES US LOL! ♥ MS. KANDRA IS THE FUNNIEST TEACHER! ♥ SHE USES ALL THESE WORDS LIKE "KRUNK" THAT I DIDN'T EVEN KNOW WHEN I CAME HERE ♥ YOU HAVE TO ADMIRE HOW SHE HOLDS HERSELF ♥ SHE SHOWS ALL HER LOVE TO YOU EVERY MOMENT ♥ SHE IS ALWAYS WILLING TO OPEN UP AND TREAT US IN A LOVING, FUNNY, KIND AND RESPECTFUL WAY ♥ SHE ALWAYS KEEPS A SMILE ON YOUR FACE EVEN WHEN YOU'RE UPSET ♥ I LOVE THIS LADY TO DEATH ♥ SHE IS LIKE A SISTER TO ME ♥ I LOVE EVERY BIT OF HER! ♥ SHE'S A COOL PERSON AND A GREAT MOTHER TO HER TWO BEAUTIFUL DAUGHTERS, SOMETHING I WILL BE ONE DAY ♥ IT BRIGHTENS UP MY DAY JUST TO SEE HER FACE ♥ SHE IS BEAUTIFUL ♥ THREE WORDS – "OFF 'DA CHAIN ♥ SHE'S A GREAT MOTHER AND A BEAUTIFUL ONE, TOO ♥ YOU HAVE A SPECIAL GIFT FOR HISTORY – DON'T LET ANYONE TAKE IT FROM YOU! ♥ MS. KANDRA SHINES JUST LIKE THE STARS! ♥

Sometimes what people say and think should matter, especially when it's something that could propel an individual into the next chapter of their life. Initially, I believed I was the one teaching when, in fact, the girls taught me a thing or two nearly every day.

Work as if God Signs Your Paycheck

I found myself in a major pit stop after graduating from UF. I couldn't seem to find a job so I did what I had to do to make ends meet. I secured a second job as a part-time custodian at a healthcare call center. Yes, I was a janitor with an advanced degree, but it was just another pit stop.

The lesson at that juncture in my life was that custodians have the gift of cleaning, listening, and discerning. I knew that one day a custodian would come to empty my trash can and I would treat them with dignity and respect. There were days I would go into the office around 5 p.m., start emptying cans and I'd feel invisible by many people who worked until later.

I would take the girls with me to clean the building because we stayed too far across town for me to leave them at home. So they'd sit at one of the desks and do their homework. When they finished, I'd give them gloves and a garbage bag to help me empty trash cans. They were tickled because I'd give them $5 for helping Mommy out.

The 14,000 square foot facility had so many bathrooms and garbage cans that I couldn't count them all. Not to mention that I had to vacuum the entire building– changing outlets every 10-12 feet. I worked three nights a week after I left PACE. It paid $7.25 an hour, but every little bit helped. The building was spotless when we left, especially after their office parties that resulted in 10-15 plus huge bags of garbage being carried to the dumpster.

One of the chief executives often worked late. I'd always walk into his office with a smile and ask how he was doing. One day he turned from his chair and said to me, "You seem smart, you should consider taking a trade at City College." City College was a local vocational school/career college. I smiled and said I would consider it. A few weeks later, he asked me if I thought about what he said. I'd had a terrible day because by the time I arrived home from PACE and picked up the girls, our lights had been disconnected. This was a Wednesday and payday wasn't until Friday. So I had to float a check to make sure the lights were turned back on the same day.

My response to Mr. Executive was: "Sir, I have a master's degree from UF in communications, but I can't seem to find a full-time job to support me and my family." He looked at me as if he saw a ghost. I emptied his garbage can and kept working.

The next week the owner of the janitorial company called me into the office and asked for the keys. He said I didn't make a good fit for the job—meaning I was overqualified on paper; I played the role to get the job. My grandmother would have been proud because she instilled in all of her grandchildren to be good at everything we put our hands to. I dummied down for that job and played them like a fiddle so that I could feed my children.

Nonetheless, this man recognized the greatness in me, and just because I was a janitor it didn't change who I was or my destiny, which is why we can't afford to turn a pit stop into a final destination. Know what you are really made of, and remain focused.

"If a man is called to be a street sweeper, he should sweep streets even as Michelangelo painted, or Beethoven composed music, or Shakespeare wrote poetry. He should sweep streets so well that all the hosts of heaven and Earth will pause to say, here lived a great street sweeper who did his job well." ~Dr. Martin Luther King, Jr.

In other words, Dr. King was simply saying work as you are working unto the Lord.

Chapter Five

Pray for the F's and G's

When your back is against the wall, pray for the three F's and expect answers from the two G's. ~ Kandra Albury

The three F's helped me to keep my focus while in the pit stop and here's what I ask God for in the following order:

First, I asked God for *faith* to make it through, knowing if anyone could supply my needs He surely would. Then I prayed for the *finances* to pay my bills, and if the finances didn't show up on time... I asked God for *favor* with the customer service representative. If all else failed I floated a check and prayed about that, too.

When I needed an answer, I went to *God* and I searched *Google*—one way or the other, I received an answer to my question or problem. Sometimes, I researched to satisfy my yearning for knowledge. I also explored potential companies that I wanted to land an interview with. I researched new words, recipes, home remedies and more. Research is a gift I stumbled upon when I opened myself up to gift of education… it empowered me and I empowered others.

My hope and faith remained stretched and pressed. Every month there were more days than dollars to pay the bills. I prayed for bills to be lowered or my income to increase via child support or by a new job paying a decent salary.

There wasn't much money for entertainment or extras— just the necessities. However, God gave me a special neighbor by the name of Ms. Rita. Her 90-something year-old mother lived with her. Whenever she went to the store, she would pick me up a gallon of milk, a loaf of bread or a dozen of eggs. She would also order a large pizza on Friday nights and call the girls over to pick up the rest. She made it her business to buy something sweet for the girls too. Even though Ms. Rita called me *Tandra* and not Kandra, I was always thankful, because she looked out for me and the girls. She was undeniably heaven-sent.

While I was a single mom, I learned to hustle. I made business cards and flyers for the man who owned a local garlic crab business, and I made business cards for another man who sold knockoff purses. I created and printed everything on my home computer.

On several occasions I couldn't see my way, but God navigated the use of my gifts and talents to make a way. I brought home $436 biweekly and had to manage the following bills:

- Rent- $475
- Lights and water- $157
- Car - $336
- Car insurance- $96
- After school care- $75 per week
- Phone and dial up internet – $125
- Cell phone added to home phone - $45 (200 minutes)
- Groceries - $75 per week

My grandmother often proclaimed, "God always knows what you need before you need it." Although my bills were late, it was seldom that they didn't get paid.

Remember what you pray for…

"Therefore I tell you, whatever you ask for in prayer, believe that you have received it, and it will be yours. And when you stand praying, if you hold anything against anyone, forgive them, so that your Father in heaven may forgive you your sins."

Mark 11:24-25, *NIV*

Chapter Six

And It Shall Surely Come to Pass

When I initially moved to Gainesville, I met a genuinely nice young lady at a local church that I visited. She was married and had two small children, a girl and a boy. Somehow we lost contact with each other but about three years later, our paths crossed again at a different church. This time she was with a different man who wasn't her husband. She had that *'just married'* glow. She wore a huge powder pink hat with a matching suit. She introduced me to her new husband after service. He was fine and happened to be a bodybuilder. I remember during service saying this little prayer… "Lord, just like you gave her another chance, please God do the same for me, and please make my husband fine like hers, Amen."

During my last semester at UF, I met this funny-looking guy in the computer lab by the name of James. We initially met via email, due to my incessant issues with formatting my thesis. The first time I entered *his* lab, I immediately noticed his bald-head and glasses; he looked like Gandhi. He wore a conservative blue shirt, a tie, and dark gray slacks. His glasses told me that my visits to the lab would be "strictly business" because his second set of eyes were the line in the sand for me. I always thought if a man wore glasses he "couldn't see me right." I was desperate for help with formatting my paper. I wanted to get it done and over with so that I could move on with my life.

James was extremely smart, patient and kind. He opened doors for me… and that was something I was not accustomed to [chivalry wasn't dead]. He was God-sent because all I wanted to do was finish my thesis and attain my goal of relocating to Chicago to become a producer with Harpo Studios.

One day [as fate would have it], just the two of us were in the lab when he said, "My parents always want me to fix their computers, but seldom come to my bodybuilding competitions." I thought to myself, "Yeah right." I kept right on typing. I thought it was strange that he was always eating chicken and broccoli when I visited the lab. He later revealed that he was carb cycling for the Mr. Gainesville Bodybuilding Competition.

He then asked me if I wanted to see something, I said sure. So I stepped into his cubicle and he showed a photo of himself in these blue posing trunks. I was pleasantly surprised! I asked if he used Photoshop to put his face on *that* body. He retorted no and asked me to squeeze his bicep… it was solid as a rock!

Our conversation continued and I told him about my girls. He thought I had four children because I called Kendriana *"Drea"* and Kenisha *"Myra."* James and I fatefully became quite fond of each other.

After I graduated, he asked me to lunch so we could celebrate. We dated for a year, became engaged in 2004, and married in December of 2005. He was the pot of gold at the end of my rainbow!

The ending of this chapter in my life reminded me of the story of Joseph who was thrown into a pit by his brothers. The story unfolded with Joseph being thrown into prison, becoming ruler over the prison, and ultimately King. His pit experience, [14 toilsome years] prepared him for *his* palace. Please keep in mind, when we remain persistent while in the pit, we will run head-on into our God ordained purpose.

I had to be at that particular college at that appointed time to have met [and betrothed] my life partner.

Chapter Seven
Favor Doesn't Exempt, It Qualifies

"Keep this Book of the Law always on your lips; meditate on it day and night, so that you may be careful to do everything written in it. Then you will be prosperous and successful." Joshua 1:8, NIV

I believe favor is a reward granted by God for consistently living a righteous lifestyle. When we live a righteously, not a perfectly, God's favor is inevitable. When we persistently go above and beyond for righteousness sake, God insistently goes out of His way to grant advanced provision, protection, and elevation. He will strengthen us supernaturally to fulfill His purpose for our lives. Favor is for life and we experience elevated favor when seasons of overflow occur.

However, favor *doesn't* exempt us from life trails such as temptation, addictions, job loss, divorce, foreclosure, or repossessions. In fact, favor qualifies us for the miraculous that exposes us to supernatural connections, wisdom and promotion. Keep in mind that we were designed for God's purpose to glorify him and to reach others by sharing our testimonies.

Additionally, favor keeps things in perspective and qualifies us as effective kingdom ambassadors. Most importantly, favor liberates us!

I have heard people state, "Living a Christian lifestyle is no walk in the park!" I immediately pondered, "Well, why should I live for God *if* I'm still going to catch hell? Now I understand that salvation was never a ploy to fail or frustrate us, but to free us and bring us into a place of fully trusting God for *everything*...from our next breath to a lifetime of good health and wealth. We must develop a desire to be one of God's ambassadors by leading, loving and allowing our light to shine in everything we do, everywhere we go, and with everyone we encounter. Our light is intensified as we persevere through trials, because they equipped us with wisdom and stamina to experience victorious living. For each trial that we endure, our light goes from that of a night light, to a flash light, to a flood light, to street lights then to a city of lights that rests upon a hill.

On several occasions, I was asked if I were Greek. At that time, I had no idea what being "Greek" was until my facial expression prompted a young lady to explain after asking me about my affiliation with a sorority. She asked, "Are you a Delta?" Now I knew what that was because she used a specific organization's name. I told her that I wasn't affiliated with any sorority at that particular time. I was extended several invitations to pledge with various sororities, but never did until the Spring of 2012… I pledged Theta Phi Sigma, a Christian sisterhood. When I was invited to be a part of this organization, I immediately noticed that the rest of the ladies and I all had the same thing in common: class, grace, style and genuine love in our hearts. These ladies were different and unique. My "nice nasty" radar didn't detect a rat in the room.

See, when favor is upon you, nothing about you is average. There's something about you and that something is the love of God that radiates from the inside out. Sometimes having favor means being lonely, but even in that God will place covenant friends and family members in your circle. Favor doesn't come easy; I believe that you're either born with it or your find it with God along your journey in life. Favor principles can be taught, but it surely cannot be bought because it is a special reward given by God himself.

There are so many people in biblical times as well as today who have found favor with God. From Mary, Jesus' mother (Luke 1:30) and David the Sheppard boy turned king (I Chronicles 17:16), to Moses, the stutterer turned eloquent speaker and the brains behind the Ten Commandments (Exodus 34:28). He also delivered the most complacent, complaining, fearful group of people from the hands of their ruthless leader Pharaoh (Exodus 33:11-13) – they all found favor with God.

Oprah was fired from a television job, Michael Jordan didn't make his high school basketball team and Jennifer Hudson was sent home from American Idol, but when favor knows your address, what you are purposed to do will come forth with ease, passion and commitment. I believe when we love without conditions, favor is bestowed upon us. Today, conditions may include only loving those who agree with your lifestyle, who look or act like us or only embracing those who support our political or religious ideologies. Romans 12:9, NIV reads: *"Love must be sincere. Hate what is evil; cling to what is good."*

"The next time someone rolls their eyes at your blessings, remember that they were not a part of the process that qualified you for the favor."

~Kandra C. Albury

TYPES OF PEOPLE YOU WILL MEET WHILE EMBRACING FAVOR AND FREEDOM:

While going through life, we are destined to meet interesting people. Some of them are purposed to be there for the long haul while others were only meant for a short ride. Nonetheless, I have encountered three types of people on my journey to receiving favor with God: beraters, paraders, and tailgaters. Their personality traits are different, but if their behaviors are studied long enough... they can be categorized without using negative stereotypes.

The Berater:

Beraters nitpick and quickly find fault; they are also pessimistic. These individuals could derail or delay you reaching your destination if you are not careful. When you share your dreams with beraters, their purpose is to pick it apart. They will start doubting and questioning the potential of your vision. They will ask how you are going to do this, that and the other without offering any solutions. Some will go as far as picking up the phone and calling another doubter or doubters who carry the same energy as they do. Now these individuals gave up on their dreams long time ago and have settled for mediocrity or gave in to the "age factor". They listen to the whispers of the enemy and believe their time has "passed." They seldom see beyond their current situations and prey on the weak. They have natural vision but sorely lack spiritual vision that leads to genuine peace and true prosperity. Their goal is to subject those around them to the spirit of fear and doubt. Beraters easily dismiss a multimillion-dollar business idea because their visions start with their eyes instead of their minds. They have hidden motives and false intentions. When your conscience speaks to you about them— listen the first time. They can make a relationship both spiritually and physically straining.

If you close the door on beraters, celebrate their absence in your life. I am confident someone else would love to sharpen iron with you!

When my husband and I started our business, I was unemployed. In fact, I had been terminated from a job that I enjoyed because I was helping others discover their purpose.

Sometimes God does things on his terms because he knows as human beings we have the tendency to become satisfied with "just enough". Remember, God is the divine orchestrator of all things. Sometimes it takes a termination to lead us to the path where we will discover dormant gifts, talents and purpose.

During my period of unemployment, I prayed to God for direction. I voluntarily secluded myself and collected unemployment... until a young lady at my church asked me to plan her wedding from start to finish. Consequently, one day following her wedding, I asked, "Lord, what will you have me to do?" He instructed me to write down everything I had done for this bride and I did, then I showed my husband and asked if he'd be my photographer and of course he said yes. I researched business plans and wrote one for our professional event planning company called *Events by Kandra*. No one would give us a loan to implement our business so we stepped out on faith and bought a camera, built our own website, designed and purchased business cards, developed branding, bought signage for our cars, and we were invited to a few free bridal shows as a vendor. It was all part of God's plan. While doing all of this, I didn't tell anyone *except* my mom, and I instructed her not to tell anyone either.

At the time, I knew that I had some closet beraters and I didn't want anyone talking me out of this next move. *Events by Kandra* has been going strong since 2007 and we've photographed and planned countless weddings and maternity photo shoots.

Before separating from beraters, ask yourself, "What value have they brought to the relationship?" It shouldn't take long to assess their impact. People come and go; relationships change *but* focus on those individuals who add value to your life. Seriously reconsider individuals that constantly benefit from you, but reciprocity from them is non-existent. They are simply space holders, do not become bitter and don't stop loving them. Go ahead and free yourself from high maintenance, fake, stressful relationships.

The Parader:

Paraders are people who celebrate you at the drop of a hat. In some cases, you must look beyond your immediate family to find paraders. These people are with you during the sunny days and thunderstorms of life. They are careful how they tell you things as not to hurt your feelings *too* badly and when they do, you quickly forgive them. They'll pray alongside you and wish you well. Your kids become their nieces and nephews and vice versa. They put the colors in your rainbow and if you are really lucky, they'll be the pot of gold at the end of your rainbow. Paraders will strike up the band to celebrate you and your accomplishments as well as be there during pit stops, encouraging you to get back on the track. They genuinely want to see you just as happy and successful as they are. Their motives are pure and their friendship is constant even if you don't talk to them every day. They are the people you go up to bat for in the natural as well as the spiritual. You share your dreams and fears with them because you know it's safe to do so. They are your covenant connection… your God-ordained BFF.

The Tailgaters:

Tailgaters are too close– so close that they have warped vision. They live in the natural yet expect spiritual manifestations. They operate in the flesh verses the spirit and lack self-control.

These tailgaters aren't the ones you see outside a sporting event, they are more like the people you experience in traffic while riding in the middle lane on a three-lane highway.

They are in the wrong lane and travel way too close. They believe that if God blessed you a certain way they, too, should receive their blessing in a similar fashion. They'll examine your life and then become frustrated when things don't happen in a timely manner in their lives. Tailgaters become so close, until they begin to compare themselves *to you*. Comparing one's life to another is dangerous because it causes us to minimize our accomplishments or write them off as insignificant. Tailgaters fail to ask God for a vision for their own life. Tailgaters tend to be envious of another person's greatness. Anticipate encountering numerous tailgaters… destiny has a tremendous platform, but everyone tagging along will not fit!

Tailgaters live under superficial conditions. Be very careful when you come across tailgaters because they can sense your insecurities and will capitalize on them. So, here's how tailgaters should be handled, stay in *your* lane, let *them* pass, and pray *they* find direction and strength to discover their own gifts, talents and purpose.

Make no apologies for the favor God has crowned you with because countless sacrifices have been made, *your* ransom is priceless. The cost reflects striving through rough days, bouncing back from the bad days, and facing each storm because rainbows *always* appear when the inclement weather subsides.

We are to be like a tree planted by a river of water. The growing process is how we develop unshakeable faith, which leads to unjustifiable favor. I believe Christ represents the water and as He waters our spiritual roots, we flourish by growing up and branching out… out of self, fear, debt, people and excuses. *Please note*, once we're planted in the right place… we become an invaluable resource to our spouses, family, friends, co-workers and our communities. People know when you are favored by God. Some will even have enough nerve to roll their eyes at your blessings and fail to acknowledge that they were not a part of the process that qualified you for the favor.

Favor is granted during the process and at the end of our trials because we choose not to abandon Godly character under pressure. When we are disciplined and faithful, it produces unexplainable blessings. So, whatever you do, don't expect others to understand *your* end results. To them, your blessings are much like missing the first 15 minutes of a movie, which is when plot is revealed. When we miss the first 15 minutes of a movie we are always left wondering what we missed and have difficulty following the storyline.

Understand this… some people will gravitate towards you and some will envy you and walk away. Expect to lose some friends; some may even grow distant because they won't be able to embrace the newness of your favor factor.

"Some people spend way too much time trying to figure out what "IT" is about you when "IT" (divine favor) has already been settled in heaven!"

~Kandra C. Albury

"When God is in you… He will shine through you."

~Kandra C. Albury

Chapter Eight

Choose Love and Go Out of Your Way to Express It

We are living in a time when love has become a hot commodity. People look for it in the strangest places and ways; it's often misused or inaccurately defined. The true definition of love has become tainted by the need for being accepted. People go places or associate with only a certain class of people in a desperate attempt to feel love and acceptance. However, love is an act that's done without any ulterior motives or expected paybacks. Love is what love does from the heart.

My grandmother baked pies and gave them away (and it wasn't a holiday or special occasion), it was her expression of love. My grandfather grew fruit and vegetables, then he drove around town like he was in a parade (slow enough to pull over when someone called) and he gave away the produce. The best part of my grandparents' legacy is how they put love into action by releasing what was in their hands so that God faithfully released what was in His. They left an indelible mark on my life because so much of who I am today is because of who they were to me.

One-year money was tight as the Christmas holiday approached. I decided to shift my family's focus; so I called City Rescue Mission and asked if we could serve the homeless on Christmas Day. I completed some paperwork and an orientation via the telephone. I ran the idea by James and we broke the news to the girls. Consequently, after we opened gifts and ate sweet potato pie for breakfast (our holiday tradition), we drove to downtown Jacksonville to the shelter.

As we neared the shelter, we saw people sleeping on the streets and in the midst of the drizzling and wintery cold rain; my eyes swelled with tears. I desperately tried to constrain my tears as we went inside. We immediately washed up, put on gloves, aprons, and started preparing plates. For three hours, we fixed plates nonstop; we put down hot meals and disposed of the empty plates. The three hours felt like thirty minutes. We served people of all races, ages and genders. Several of them prayed deep prayers before they ate.

For the first time in my, I intimately interacted with these often-invisible people…but God loved them just the same as He loved me; and I was overwhelmed with the love of

God on *that* day. As I relished in that of God's love, I overheard one of the men tell another gentleman how blessed he felt just to have food and fellowship with others! When we left, we all said we'd do it again. The experience taught all of us to count our blessings because no matter how bad we believed our situation was, we saw firsthand how it could be worse.

Little did I know that three years later my daughters' father would call that same shelter home.

"The process doesn't change your blessings it builds your endurance and conditions your heart to receive them in God's timing."

~Kandra C. Albury

WHAT'S IN YOU WILL COME OUT OF YOU

My mom always said, "What is in you will come out of you." If darkness is on the inside of you, darkness will beam from you. If light is on the inside of you, light will project from you.

My grandmother served on the Mother's Board at Mt. Moriah Baptist Church and would sing "This Little Light of Mine" with authority (off-key and loud enough for the heavens to hear her). She sang it as if she was commanding heaven's light to shine upon her at that very moment. She would sing: "Everywhere I go, I'm going to let it shine, all in my home, I'm going to let it shine. All on my job I'm going to let it shine, let it shine, let it shine, let it shine!"

My granny never could carry a note, but she tried, *emphatically*. She lived the words of the song. She fed the hungry, taught us how to cook, sew, wrap gifts, and make a bed better than any hotel maid. Her love for sharing and empowering others deemed her *that city that sat upon a mountaintop.*

One of the best words of advice from my grandmother, was not to move too fast. After having my first daughter, she showed up to my two-bedroom, one bath duplex inspected Drea from head to toe and said, "What a fine baby, but don't you take yourself too fast or you'll have a setback and end up back in the hospital. Once those doctors cut on you (perform a C-section), you have to let yourself heal before moving around too much." She'd call me daily to make sure I wasn't out running errands or moving around too much. She said I needed to stay in the house for eight weeks, but that was a little too long for me!

I applied her "setback" advice in other areas of my life. It helped me to think thoroughly before moving too quickly because I didn't want to suffer a setback, especially when it came to relationships and dating.

My grandmother taught my cousins [male and female] and I domestic tasks and how to spell first words, *'cat and chicken…'* Unfortunately, she also called us the N-word. She used this epithet so much when I was a kid that it was *just* another word, *until a white person used it*. I'm not sure why my grandmother called us that, but it may have had something to do with there being 15-20 grandkids running around the house at a time that she couldn't remember all of our names. To her credit, she only called us the N-word when we misbehaved or seriously aggravated her.

Little did she know that I wasn't going to be her nigger and I sure wasn't going to be any white person's nigger. I was destined to be who God purposed me to be… awesome! However, there is no doubt in my mind that she loved every one of us and wanted us to have a better life than she and my grandfather because she constantly reinforced the value of a good education. She wanted us to be smart and survive in the world.

Chapter Nine

Trauma Produces Tenacity and Builds Our Faith

Even as a child, God answered my prayers. One unforgettable evening, my mom was picked by the police for writing a worthless check. The officers showed up to our house in an unmarked car. The uniformed officers asked who was the oldest to see who was of legal age to watch us while they hauled my Mom off to the county jail. I believe my oldest sister may have been 14 at the time. My aunts who lived next door showed up to see what was going on. They put my Mom in the back of the car and sped off. I went in my bedroom that I shared with my oldest sister and fell to my knees and prayed that God brought my mom back home, and He did. In fact, she was back home that same night.

On another occasion, my mom sent me in the local corner store to pick up a check that had bounced. I went in the store, asked for the owner and they sent me straight to the back, past the meat counter, to his office. It was dark but there was a lamp on his desk shining light on his face. I gave him the money rolled up and he opened his drawer and gave me the check. I turned and walked away. Before I exited, he said "Hey little girl, tell ya momma don't let this happen again." I said, "Yes, sir" and quickly hurried away. I got back in the front seat of the car and told momma what he said; she never said a word as we drove off. I knew then that checks were the devil, especially if people came looking for you to straighten out the situation.

These experiences made me appreciate my mom even more because I knew the sacrifices she made were to keep our family together.

"Sometimes we go through things that build our spiritual muscle that prepares us for what's down the road, around the corner and up the hill."

~Kandra C. Albury

FIVE KEY WAYS TO COMMUNICATE WITH GOD AND FIND FAVOR:

"Keep in mind that how you go through your tests, and setbacks determine your next measure of favor."

~Kandra C. Albury

Speak it. God said let there be light and there was light! Open your mouth and refuse to get lockjaw... when stressful situations manifest - speak life!

Write it. Habakkuk 2:2 instructs us to write the vision. I urge you to write a vision for your life and don't forget to speak blessings over your children (in writing).

Live by faith. Hebrews 11:6 clearly states that without faith it is impossible to please God and anyone who comes to him must believe that he exists. Habakkuk 2:4 also states that the just shall *live* by faith.

Pray about it. I Thessalonians 5:17 instructs us to pray without ceasing. When we pray without ceasing, the lighter our burdens become. Once we realize that God won't only supply our needs (Philippians 4:19) but will also give us our heart's desires, (Psalms 37:45), then our faith and measure of favor increases.

I believe we are all favored and when a season of favor comes, we experience elevated favor.

Listen for God's voice. "My sheep listen to my voice; I know them, and they follow me." John10:27, KJV

Make quiet time, even if it means turning off the radio while driving, silencing the cell phone for 15 minutes…make time to silence the noise. Use the quiet time to thank God, then speak life over every dormant situation. We must remove expiration dates from our blessings then speak and believe for life-long blessings. We should even expect encore blessings, expanded blessings and unexpected blessings.

Start by decreeing wonderful things to unfold in your life by reciting the following affirmations:

- Let there be love, peace, joy and happiness in my life for the remainder of my life!

- Let there be generational blessings on my life for the remainder of my life!

- Let generational curses be broken over my life for the rest of my life!

- Let there be great employment and entrepreneurial opportunities in my life for the remainder of my life!

- Let every dormant gift arise and flow freely in my life for the remainder of my life!

- Let there be increase in my life for the remainder of my life!

- Let there be divine revelation in my life for the remainder of my life!

- Let me pray according to God's will in my life, my family's life for the rest of our lives!

- Let there be Godly wisdom applied in my life for the remainder of my life!

Now call some things forth! Feel free to write them down too.

Let there be _____ in my life for the remainder of my life.

"Train your brain to tame your tongue."

~Kandra C. Albury

Favor Commandments to Gain Peace and Prosperity

- Believe in the power of God

- Pray and pray often; believe what you pray for can and will happen

- Appreciate the goodness of God (no matter how great or small)

- Put biblical principles into practice

- Maintain balance and prioritize

- Do not abandon Godly character during stressful situations and use self-control

- Seek the truth for yourself (Remember the two G's);

- Accept trials with grace, perseverance and a positive mental attitude

- Unclog your mind and life/take inventory of things and people who must go

- Be a good steward over everything and everyone you are responsible for

- Celebrate your growth and successes and the growth and successes of others

✦ Abandon negativity (emotions, people and behaviors); and give of yourself gifts, talents and resources to others in need

"Love is most powerful when we put it into action-- showing it— receiving it—believing in it!"

Every time you want to think a negative thought, intercept it with a positive one and speak it! Every time someone speaks the opposite of the vision that you have for your life, position yourself to overcome their falsehoods with your reality.

I remember when a relative told me to quit college after giving birth to my second daughter. In fact, she said I should quit because I wasn't going to finish. I thought it was a very mean thing for her to say, but I was determined to make life better for my family.

When people speak everything except life over you, the best thing you can do is prove to them who your God is. I didn't have a rebuttal to my relative's comment, I simply tapped into that inner strength– that being God and his strength, which have always pushed me to discover and rediscover some inner strength that I never knew I possessed.

You have to put action behind your prayers and your faith. Only then will you find yourself closer to your destiny!

Speak the opposite of what you feel, believe or see. I also encourage you to find a scripture or motivational material that speaks the opposite of what's challenging you. Expect what you say and write to happen.

I encourage you to speak blessings over your life then start moving in the direction of your goals. Between you and your determination and God with His infinite power, your naysayers will be silenced. Send your enemies some popcorn, a thank you note and a box tissue because *the* movie, starring you, will have a happy ending!

I remember when I had my first job after graduating with my bachelor's degree from the University of North Florida. I submitted a writing sample to the Palatka Daily News and was hired instantly. The editor said there was something about *my* article. So, he called and asked me to come in for an interview. I dressed up and put on my interview face.

I was excited and covered everything from city and county government to environmental news and courts. I was honored when one of the editors asked me to write about my mom for a Mother's Day piece. I thought that would be easy so I agreed. I talked about how she raised five children as a single mom and the values she instilled in us. Some of those being: respect of self and adults, education and to love God.

I ended the article with the vision that I had to attend UF and major in mass communications. A short while later, I graduated from UF with a master's degree in mass communications. I spoke with my attending UF advisor twice– once after attending cheerleading camp and when I wrote it in the article.

When my daughter was in middle school, her behaviors was noticeably problematic and the school administrators threatened to put her in an alternative school. I told her, "You will straighten up and you will finish where you started." On the day that we arrived at the alternative school to meet with the dean, he stepped outside of his office and said: "For some reason we can't find her paperwork anywhere," looking confused. "I guess this is your second chance, young lady."

I told my husband two weeks before Christmas in 2009 that the Lord was going to bless him with a free car. James, being the person he is (one who needs a glimpse of a blessing before believing), mumbled something. I said, "OK."

Three weeks later, my father-in-law called while I was at work. When I answered he said, "I was getting some service done on my car here at the dealership and I saw a car identical to mine and wanted to know if you think James would want it. I sold a portion of my stocks and paid cash for it." I chimed in, "Are you kidding me? Of course, he would." James' vehicle had no heat or AC and could barely go. He dressed like an Eskimo during the winter and came home drenched in sweat in the summer.

These are just a few examples of the positive things that *will* happen when visions are spoken or written, be careful negatively spoken/written things will manifest negatively.

As a child, my mother told me and my siblings that our house was the "poor house." I'm not sure if she said that to keep us from being wasteful or to confirm the fact that we were not wealthy. Either way, her words were ingrained in my mind.

I frequently told my daughters similar things to keep them from being careless. I'd say…

- Hey, turn off those lights, this is the poor house!

- Close the door, the air is on, this is the poor house!

- Don't eat all the food at once, this is the poor house; and

- Turn off that bathwater, this is the poor house!

I professed these things almost every day not knowing that I was speaking death on my life as well as my children's lives. Unknowingly, I rejected prosperity due to my ignorance and embraced poverty because of my upbringing. Then one day I heard a minister say: "There's power of life and death in the tongue." I thought about it and was deeply saddened for exposing my children to a mentality of lack. From that point on, I trained myself to say our house was rich and full of everything we need! My girls smiled every time I declared it.

Try it, say: "I am wealthy, healthy, and full of joy with more than enough. I am on my way to greatness and nothing or no one can change this!" Feels good, doesn't it? It should because wholeness and plenty are what God desires for us!

Chapter Ten

Don't Scrub the Mission

When I was a little girl, my siblings and I were always fascinated by the space program, and our teachers escorted us outside to watch the shuttle launches. Whenever there was inclement weather, NASA officials scrubbed the mission. The possibility of rain always caused me to worry. I still remember the day that the Challenger explosion happened. School was closed because it was unusually cold—now that didn't happen often in Florida, but every now and again there was a hard freeze. On this particular day, NASA representatives decided not to abort the mission. My brothers were outside watching and I was parked in front of the TV. When the shuttle exploded in mid-air, I was shocked and thought to myself, "Maybe they should have scrubbed that launch."

Those aboard the Challenger were on a mission. I'm sure the astronauts had experienced scrubs at some point in the past. That morning, they boarded the shuttle as ambitious human beings and died as heroes. Many of them lived their dream by exploring the universe beyond the sky, clouds, moon and stars as we know it. I'm sure they were nervous or even afraid. I am sure the teacher had her concerns as it was her first mission. The crew put countless hours into preparation, and I'm sure none of them woke up with an attitude of *not* making it happen. They all showed up, suited up, and boarded the shuttle as if the mission was going to be like any other. They listened to the countdown and launched into Earth's atmosphere, not knowing it would be their final mission.

Even as we are on our earthly missions, we must realize how important it is *not to* scrub or abort our missions because we never know when our final mission will be. Each smaller mission leads to a greater one. Sometimes we have to endure the stormy weather (challenges in relationships, finances, careers and health) so that God can launch us into our next assignment. In every storm, there is a test that we must pass; if we pass the test we are more prepared for our next mission. However, we must decide during the preparation period whether we will allow life's storms to serve to our demise or contribute to our determination as we strive to reach our destiny.

I use the analogy of a storm, but the Bible refers to this process as the refiner's fire. I say the longer we stay in the fire, the stronger, smarter and shinier we become, just like metal.

When I was in the middle of a difficult time at work once, a friend of mine by the name of Sabrina Williams sent me a text titled "Stand Your Ground." I received the text as I drove into the garage. I raised my eyebrows because I needed to hear some encouraging words regarding this stressful situation. I realized what I had experienced the last two days was designed to bring depression, sadness, frustration, and gloom. I wanted to quit, but refused to walk away. I did not want to retake *that* test in the very near future. The whispers of the enemy clouded my mind… "you have your own business, your husband has a decent job, walk into your boss's office and give her a piece of your mind."

But… I prayed, utilized self-control, and forced myself to continue going to work *on time* and working the *full shift*. I almost shed tears but I refused to cry. I had been around this mountain before and I had the bruises to remind me not to march around it again!

Earlier that day, I was called into the office by a senior leader who simply wanted to nick pick. I was demeaned, questioned, and undermined. This meeting occurred on a Monday and my boss's birthday was two days later.

Please know that if we keep failing a test, God will keep giving it to us. He'll give us little quizzes, too, to make sure we are prepared for *the* big test. I remember a word a pastor spoke and it was simple: "We were not born to retreat; we were born to attack" [in the spiritual realm - II Corinthians 10:4 explains how to win every battle].

God reminded me of a time when many of my close family members and friends missed my wedding. I was deeply saddened and hurt. I wrote thank you cards to send to those who attended and God whispered, "You have to send a card to those who *didn't* attend as well." I did so… *in tears*.

Thus, I found myself in the *same* situation when it came to this matter so I asked, "Lord, do I have to buy a card and attend my boss's birthday luncheon?" He whispered, "*Remember…*" So not only did I sign the office birthday card, next to my birthday wish I added a glittery sticker. I also bought a personal card for my boss, added another sticker and signed: "Your next lunch is on me, let me know when."

Ninety-percent of the time people don't have a problem with us, their problem is with the favor that is upon our life. In many cases they are wrestling with their own insecurities.

We must understand the importance of asking God to give us a heart that allows us to freely and genuinely forgive. When we grow into this place, we release an elevated level of blessings and favor on our life… don't believe it, just try it. *God's waiting… and so is His favor!*

"Serve yourself and others notice about who you really are. When you don't know your value, others will gladly help you determine it. Be warned— you may feel shortchanged or well compensated—you decide."

~Kandra C. Albury

How are you rooted?

When I was a child, my birthday wish was always, always to be rich. I'd wish for a million dollars. As I've gotten older and put things into perspective, I have learned that wealth requires being a good steward over the things we currently have and being content in our mind, while yet striving to reach our goals. God shows up when we are productive and good stewards of our time and resources.

I remember buying my first Coach purse; I waited about a year before going to the Coach store and purchasing one. From time-to-time, I looked at different ones online. I finally made a trip to the Coach Outlet. The store was bustling with delighted women modeling the latest handbags, scarves and hats. I was a little disconnected from all of the excitement and I wasn't quite sure why. I looked at four or five bags, and then asked a sales associate to assist me. I purchased "the purse", a matching wristlet and a scarf. My new purse was sweet and sophisticated and Lord knows it was big enough to accommodate a kitchen sink. I paid for my purchase and headed to the car. Once in the car, I realized that I had been carrying my Target purse like it was a Coach. The value wasn't in the purse, but *within* me.

As I drove home, I thought about how my mom used to tell us to be grateful for what we had. I realized that I became grateful for the no-name purses that I carried like a $200 designer bag so when I purchased my first Coach, it was like I was carrying just another purse.

The same thing happened with my dream-nightmare car [a 2005 Acura RL]; my husband and I purchased it in 2006 as an investment for our event planning business. I loved the car so much that I had gone to the dealership and sat in one several years earlier. I had my eye on the car when Acura replaced the Legend with the RL. It was a beauty; black with camel-colored interior. It had about 60K miles on it when we purchased it. I didn't care about the miles because I thought, *"Hey, it's an Acura nothing could possibly go wrong with it."* Well, in two years the air conditioning went out to the tune of $1,800, all of the leather interior on the arm rests and door panels peeled ($635 repair), the stereo system stopped working ($1,500 repair- under warranty-thank goodness) and a joint failed ($985 repair). After a couple of years, we quickly realized that we were driving a money pit; not to mention the low-profile tires were $265 per tire.

I told James that God would make a way for us to pay the car off early. In 2010, I thought it would be totaled when I was rear-ended, but that didn't do it. I kept saying that the car would get paid off early. Then one day I received a call from my daughter saying a woman came by the house and dropped off a card with a phone number. I asked for the number and called it. The woman said we're with the repossession department and all accounts have to be current. I couldn't understand because my payment was 38 days past due and I had planned to make a payment *that* same week. She said all accounts have to be current in two days with the next month's payment and all late fees.

I couldn't believe what I heard; it almost sounded like a scam. So, I called James and told him what happened. We didn't get upset. I simply began searching for dream car number two, a Buick Lacrosse, and besides we only had a couple of months to pay off the car and could consider trading it in. So I checked online for a used Lacrosse and came across a dealership inquiry form and filled it out. In about 30 minutes I received a call from a young woman who took some of my information. Then 10 minutes later the manager of the dealership called me and asked what I wanted and I said I'd like a pre-owned 2010 Lacrosse. He asked if I had considered a 2012. He said they had a great sign and drive lease. I stopped him when he said lease and asked, "When you lease a car, can you buy it?" He said I had three options with a lease:

✦ Purchase the car at the end of the lease agreement;

✦ Turn the car in; or

✦ Trade it for an upgrade

I was excited and gave him my husband's phone number. James and I talked and agreed to a lease with the option to purchase at the end of the agreement. He asked what color I wanted and if I wanted leather. I was tickled because I had never owned a brand-new car. I went online and customized everything. When we picked-up the car, it was parked on the showroom floor and I didn't know that the showroom car was my car until the manager said, "By the way, Mrs. Albury, this is your car." I was numb and it was very surreal. I'm glad I didn't pull a stunt like the people you see on *The Price is Right*. The car is charcoal-colored with black leather interior, custom wheels and all the bells and whistles–exactly how I saw on Buick's website.

My grandfather's Sunday car was a Buick, my father-in-law drives a Buick, and so does my husband. When the LaCrosse came out with this particular design, I knew what I'd be investing in… a good old-fashioned American car – a name with a trusted reputation. I am a Buick girl for now and I don't know if I'll drive anything else, *but* for now I'm content.

These lessons taught me that in life, as we start to understand our value and where it lies, we will begin to put things into perspective. Don't get me wrong, there's nothing like having the finer things in life, especially if you work hard for them, but when we choose not to allow those things to define us or determine our happiness, then we've arrived at two additional benefits to prosperity, and they are joy and contentment. Contentment and joy will sustain you long after the excitement of having the new thing is gone.

I recognize joy as a long-term inner peace that isn't contingent upon life situations or what may happen; it's not about success or the lack thereof. Joy rests in the soul and we must choose to allow it to take permanent residence. No matter what, joy always prevails when we *choose* it! However, joy does not make us superhuman, but it helps us to be at peace with people, things, and situations. Best of all, when you discover it, you will ask, "So all I needed was j-o-y?" Yes, joy. If we sit still long enough to drown out the noise in life, we can easily pinpoint the causes of chaos in our lives.

The pursuit of joy must become a life mission that *should* start with owning joy, then instilling "joy values" in our children. This is accomplished by teaching them that they are invaluable in all aspects! They are a gift from God and they are destined to do great things. We must teach them that things will come and go but the love that we instill in them can last a lifetime. When we master this, we are teaching them how to build a lasting legacy that is built on love. Remember, Jesus is love.

Prune, Pray, and Allow God to Replenish…

My mom used to plant coleus every year and when they'd get tall, she'd prune them back, and suddenly, they would grow fuller and thicker.

Like coleus, some people need trimming out of our lives so that we *can* grow. In some cases, God will even place a better quality of people (fertilizer) around us to help us blossom even more.

There have been times when I felt abandoned by those closest to me. However, in my loneliness, I realized how much control I had given these individuals. I also realized how much courage it would take to regain control of my life. I've always been the celebrator and the encourager—remember I was a cheerleader, but when those whom I expected to celebrate with me on my wedding day or when I graduated college weren't there, I was crushed.

I tried to figure out why some of my closest friends and family members wouldn't support me. Was it because this was my second marriage? Maybe they didn't like the fact that my husband was Catholic? Or, did they envy my happiness? Whatever the reason, they missed out on a great day of celebration. The wedding was first class and was held at the University of Florida (where we met) and the reception was held at Steve's Café in the heart of downtown Gainesville. The food was the best in town and the venue was breathtaking.

The lack of support during these times taught me that not everyone will applaud you, and it is OK to genuinely love people from afar. Following these events, my phone calls became few. I had to learn how to move forward with the new boundaries that I put in place. The line was in the sand and at that point, I had to teach people how to treat me by truly knowing my value and closing the door to those who only came around when things were not good! Each day I got stronger and stronger, and I learned that I didn't need anyone's permission to walk in the blessings of God. I didn't need others to validate who I was or to offer their unwanted opinions or approvals. At 32, I learned it was OK to not have a circle of friends, but a square or triangle would do as long as those forming it sincerely meant well in both words and deeds.

A word to the wise: monitor the behavior patterns that surface when it's time to celebrate your accomplishments. If a pattern is questionable, then reevaluate that friendship/relationship and decide whether they belong in your inner or outer circle.

Make no apologies for the favor that is upon you, God chose us even when we couldn't conceptualize the greatness of His amazing grace.

Chapter Eleven
Take Time to Discover Your Gifts

My grandmother always said, "Be good at more than one thing." Profoundly enough, her words were biblical. The Bible says, *your gifts* will make room for you. I believe when we put ourselves in motion by operating our gift(s), we will discover every gift within us.

The key to discovering our gifts and bringing our dream(s) into reality *is* writing them down and praying for wisdom and blessings regarding them. I prayed for God to put the right people in my path and to allow me to be in the right place(s) at the right time.

Quite some time ago, my daughter Myra was asked by a friend to do her hair and makeup for prom. I knew the family struggled financially. Her mom raisied her and her two teenage siblings alone. The family didn't have transportation and lived in a two-bedroom apartment. Her brother slept on the couch and the girls slept in one of the bedrooms. I had no idea that both of my daughters' connection to the family would serve as a blessing to them. The week before the event, Myra asked if she could take some of Drea's formal dresses for her friend to choose one to wear to the prom. Myra and James took a total of five dresses for her to decide on; I didn't know she even had five dresses hanging in her closet. She chose an elegant purple gown, she looked gorgeous.

On the day of her prom, I had an event to cover for work, an appointment to help a friend put together the program for her 40th birthday, and I was supposed to meet with another friend to work on a marketing plan for her consulting business.

I felt stretched, but I knew Myra was passionate about doing hair and makeup and her friend was really depending on her. So, we went to the hair store, purchased products and Myra immediately went to work. Once she started, we discovered that there were few products and tools missing to make the style complete. I volunteered to go to the store. Her mom had just walked through the door from work and her eyes lit up because her mom typically worked late. She said she got off on time to make sure she saw her daughter before she left for prom.

Her mom and I went to a nearby store and she picked up scissors, spritz and some other household products. Then we stopped by McDonald's to purchase food for those back at the house. Myra worked on her makeup until we returned with the needed supplies. She looked beautiful.

Suddenly, her cell phone rang, her friends had arrived the planned meeting location and were waiting in their limo. One of them explained they'd be leaving soon. I felt like we were rushing Cinderella to the ball. She carefully and quickly slipped into her dress. Her hair and makeup were flawless, she looked like a princess.

I drove as fast and as safely as I could through the shopping center. I rushed out of the car shook the hand of the driver and thanked him for waiting. I stuck my head in the limo and thanked her friends for waiting. I told them to enjoy and be safe. She was glowing and looked like she didn't have a care in the world; when in fact, she had been working quite a few hours since her 18th birthday to help her mom with the bills, while managing advanced placement classes and preparing for graduation but none of that mattered because for that moment she looked and felt like royalty.

During the drive home, her mom asked me how I guided Myra in the operation of her gift. I paused and said, "She has watched me operate in my gifts through the years." I told her my girls have always been a part of everything that I've done. From preparing food for guests, to serving as the pose coordinator for our event planning business; they've always shadowed me and learned in the process how to do things with a signature touch. They know that with God nothing is impossible. They take their gifts and research various topics online to grow their gifts. Most importantly, they know that it's better to give than to receive and *to be* a blessing is a blessing.

Watching your children operate in their gifts with genuine love and passion is another reward of motherhood and righteous living. Remember that God knows the difference between a yes from the mouth and a yes from the heart. The heart's yes, lead to generational blessings and favor. God reviews our spiritual resumes to make sure we are ready for promotion because it only comes from Him.

Elementary Lesson Turned Life Lesson #2

My second-grade teacher, Mrs. Miller, read a book that I fell in love with, entitled, "The Five Chinese Brothers." The fact that I can remember the book says a lot about how the story has impacted my life.

The five brothers all looked alike and lived with their mother on the oceanside. They all had unique gifts. One could swallow an entire sea, one had an iron neck, one could stretch his legs to any length, one could not be burned, and the other could hold his breath indefinitely.

One day a little boy pleaded to go with the one who could swallow up the sea to collect pebbles at the bottom of the ocean. He warned the little boy that he had to obey and come back to shore when he signaled. Well, the boy didn't come back to shore when he signaled with his hands. He released the ocean from his jaws and the boy was never seen again.

The judge sentenced him to death. He was tried, imprisoned, and sentenced to death by way of head decapitation. The morning of the execution, he asked the judge if he could go home and say goodbye to his mother, the judge said yes. The next day the second brother with the iron neck came back in his place. Everyone came to witness the execution. The executioner gave him a blow to the neck with a sharp sword, nothing happened. He got up and took a bow; his head could not be cut off. Everyone was angry.

They then sentenced him to be drowned. When he went to bid farewell to his mother, the one with the iron neck changed places with his brother who could stretch his legs. The next day all the town people gathered at the edge of the sea to witness a boat take him out to sea and be thrown overboard. His legs stretched and stretched. He could not be drowned.

Then they brought him back to land and sentenced him to be burned. He asked the judge if he could bid his mother farewell, and the judge said yes. He went and the one who couldn't be drowned traded places with the one who couldn't be burnt. He was tied to a stake and all the townspeople stood around watching. From the flames they heard him say how pleasant it was. They crowd shouted to bring more wood. The fire grew bigger and he said it was quite comfortable. The crowd was infuriated!

Finally, they decided to smother him. On the morning of the execution, the brother who couldn't be burnt, traded places with the brother who could hold his breath indefinitely. A large brick oven had been built in the village square and stuffed with whip cream. He was stuffed into the oven. Everyone stayed there all night and vowed that they would not be tricked again. The next day they opened the door and pulled him out. He shook himself and said how nicely he slept. The judge then stepped up and said, "We've tried to get rid of you in every way possible, but somehow it can't be done…you must be innocent!" They let him go and he went home to live with his four Chinese brothers and his mother.

What fascinated me most about this story was each of them had a gift that ultimately saved each other's life. They worked together to avoid execution; they also understood the gift they all possessed. I also learned that disobedience will cost you something (remember the little boy who refused to come back but disappeared).

If we want to survive in *this* world we must recognize that some people's gifts may be different or more powerful than ours… However, we possess gift(s) that can benefit someone else [when we exercise them]. The world needs *you* and your God-given greatness! We must also appreciate the gifts and talents of those around us, better yet pray that God surrounds us with people that have gifts and talents that are different than ours; that foster hope, encouragement, and mentorship opportunities.

Since we are multipurpose beings it is our duty to discover our *other* purposes as we graciously accept our primary purpose for existing, which starts with a heart of gratitude. We never know when our gifts may reveal themselves… they could manifest at age six or sixty. We're never too young or too old to open ourselves to purposeful possibilities.

God asked Moses, "What is that in your hand?" God needed him to recognize the power within. Once we confess our connection to God, whatever we hold in our hands *will* multiply and prosper. Think about people like Dion Sanders, Will Smith, Tyler Perry, Queen Latifah, Beyoncé, Oprah Winfrey, and T.D. Jakes, just to name a few. They all are multitalented because they realized that they were equipped to master and created to conquer by operating in their primary gift that paved the way for supplementary gifts to flourish.

From mastering two professional sports (football and baseball), Sanders was nicknamed "Prime Time." Queen Latifah, Beyoncé, and Will Smith have mastered the music industry as well as the big screen. Tyler Perry, Oprah, and TD Jakes have all mastered the art of storytelling using various platforms. Oprah has also mastered network ownership and movie production. TD Jakes has mastered empowering and motivating others with his gift of dissecting scriptures and delivering messages that allow people to "get it." Additionally, he has mastered being an author, film producer, and music producer. Tyler Perry has mastered stage plays and movies that address the misconceptions about social class, abuse, and the power of forgiveness. He skillfully takes his audiences on an emotional roller-coaster ride that makes them laugh, cry, and ultimately be empowered to ponder forgiveness.

Romans 12:6-7 reads: "Having then gifts differing according to the grace that is given to us, whether prophecy, let us prophesy according to the proportion of faith; Or ministry, let us wait on our ministering: or he that teaches on teaching."

Our gifts (*plural*) will carry us through our tests, trials, and even persecution. When Jesus journeyed to the cross, He still possessed His gifts… and when He rose they were intact and miraculously indomitable.

People may attempt to shatter your self-confidence because they recognize your gifts. Don't you worry, your gifts *cannot* be taken away because they were assigned *to you* by God and they reside within you!

"The only reason you should return to a closed door is to make sure it's locked or to add some extra bolts, but whatever you do don't open the door!"

~Kandra C. Albury

Chapter Twelve

Forgiveness Isn't Optional

"And be ye kind one to another, tenderhearted, forgiving one another, even as God for Christ's sake hath forgiven you." Ephesians 4:32, KJV

Forgiveness is never petty – *it is* powerful! It empowers, uplifts, enlightens and lightens (our heavy burdens). Forgiveness allows closed doors to open and opened doors to close; whichever direction the door swings, forgiveness allows us to be at peace with the outcome. Forgiveness means we've memorialized that horrible thing, so we can live. It's choosing to exchange resentment, negative attitudes, and darkness for the light of love.

It puts us in a position to make spiritual and emotional deposits into our life as well as the lives of others. As a result of walking in forgiveness, we choose light over darkness and at this pivotal moment healing and love flow freely. Conversely, unforgiveness causes suppression, which place limits on various areas of our life; it completely stunts our growth.

After my divorce, I thought God was mad at me and I didn't think I could love again. I had to rediscover who I was and whose I was. I wanted to know where I faltered and acknowledge those places that I could improve. I was disappointed that I let my children down, failed God and myself, but as time progressed, forgiveness, healing and peace became my portion. Even during my marriage, I battled with self-esteem issues, so I was coming out of a shell and was determined not to enter another one.

I went straight from my momma's house into marriage and community college. I couldn't afford to lose my college scholarships and there was so much on the line. I was married at 19 and the marriage lasted for eight years. I had my first daughter at 20 and my second child was born 18 months later. All of this happened as I worked part time, attended college full time, sang in the choir, cared for my ailing in-laws, and prepared Sunday announcements. The need to be everything for everybody got the best of me.

Once my marriage ended, I no longer worried about meeting the expectations of so many people. My divorce was a resurrection for my mind and soul. I was a believer in God and heavily involved in my church, but I was also smothered by everyone's expectations and opinions. I needed to free myself and I found freedom in walking away from the one thing that I truly believed in… the people and things that kept me running behind social acceptance. I knew one day I would truly see the benefit of my decision and would relish in genuine joy. I prayed and faced some difficult trials, but I knew in the long run that I would be OK.

The greatest lesson I learned was the difference between joy and happiness. Joy rests in the soul and happiness is an emotion that is often contingent upon external influences. My joy was ever-present, withstanding people walking out of my life, job losses, broken relationships, and tangible things.

I also discovered that unforgiveness delayed my freedom. Unforgiveness cracks the door to negative thoughts, behavior, emotions, and setbacks. I woke up one day and chose to walk in forgiveness. I can't recall the specific prayer I prayed but I'm sure I whispered something to God and He heard me. Sometimes we simply must decide to forgive even if we choose not to confront the person that hurt us.

As an adolescent, I always wondered why my dad wouldn't spend time with me, or *just* be there. I've been married twice and wanted him to give me away both times. He never showed up, and I even offered to pay for his tuxedo, travel, and hotel accommodations. Then one day, I said to myself, *he has missed out on a great opportunity to connect with a cool person who knows how to laugh and make others laugh, one who can throw down in the kitchen, and make special things by hand—one who is simply gifted. He has short-changed himself because my children are just as amazing as I am, and he doesn't know them either.*

Then I realized that sometimes people's own shame will keep them distant, but prayer and the peace bring hope and comfort to the situation. It has been through prayer that I've overcame the rejection I felt because my father wasn't a part of my life. It was the way that my mom and grandparents loved others, that inherently taught me to keep on loving despite the cards that had been dealt to me.

So, make peace with your past *and* people – in fact, applaud them… because in return *your* future will give *you* a standing ovation. Your past hurts or mistakes didn't disqualify your future blessings– regardless of how "bad" the situation was.

God's grace is liberating and within it, condemnation does not reside. Do not allow the past to invade *your* present space and rob you of God's promises. His promises are everlasting.

Words Soothe the Soul

Whenever I have something pressing on my mind, I always write a little note. Recently, I had an epiphany regarding my relationship with my father. I was in the middle of doing something at work but took time to write this note in my journal:

"All these years, I've waited for you to say I'm sorry for not being a part of my life. Perhaps you have been waiting for me to forgive you? With that said, I forgive you, Daddy – that quickly and that easily. I release you from *my* solitary confinement." Then I wrote a letter and it went a little something like this:

Dad, I realized on Father's Day, that I had not forgiven you for abandoning us and leaving us to live a life of poverty, but it is OK because we made it. I could never pick up the phone and call you because I didn't know where to start, and maybe you didn't either. Every year when I searched for a Father's Day card for everyone else, I never could find one for you that read:

Today, I just want to say I'm sorry for missing your childhood; Daddy was a jerk. I let you down in so many ways and so many times. I didn't protect you or make you feel like a princess. How could I have missed every birthday, cheerleading tryouts, the graduations, and the births of my grandchildren?

I'm sorry I wasn't there to experience the innocence of childhood, see you off to prom, or inspect those boys that courted you. I am sorry that I wasn't there when your life was falling into pieces. I wasn't there to walk you down the aisle or dance with you on your wedding day. How I wish I could have been there to hold my grands when they were only days or a few weeks old. Will you please forgive me, baby girl? Can we start over today? If so, call me; my telephone number is _____. Believe it or not, I have a void in my life because you aren't in it. I've missed so much, but don't want to miss another moment of your life. If I don't hear from you right away, I guess that means you'll be thinking about whether you want to let me into your life now. Although you may not believe me, you have always been in my prayers, my heart, and on my mind. Daddy really is anxiously waiting to hear from you— no strings attached, just the ones that long to tie our lives and hearts together. The invitation is open. ~Virgil

How I *would* reply:

Daddy,

You've always said that you "paid your child support." Well, thank you because I'm sure it helped mom in some kind of way, be it providing a meal or some much needed clothes or shoes, but just because you paid child support it did not give you the right to dismiss yourself from my life. I graduated a total of seven times in my life (dating back to Head Start). You didn't protect me and that's been difficult to wrap my mind around because maybe, just maybe had you been there, I would not have experienced so many dark pitstops, but that's OK because those pitstops made me the woman that I am today. Daddy, your absence helped me to guard my heart and emotions, your lack of protection taught me to trust God. Trusting God taught me about His amazing grace and forgiveness. Today, I forgive you and embrace the benefits of forgiveness. May our lives be blessed regardless of how our relationship grows. I realize that three things are constant: You are my dad and I am your daughter, I love you still, and we were created to conquer, made to master, and born to beat the odds! By the way, I've enclosed some stamps in case you're not on the up-and-up with social media. Maybe we can get together soon for lunch and start there.

Love,

Kandra

"Destiny - Accepting that you will arrive at an appointed place in your future regardless of who has or hasn't been there all along. God orchestrated your life while you were growing in your mother's womb; you are a forethought, not an afterthought!"

~Kandra C. Albury

Chapter Thirteen

Fear or Faith… You Choose

Everything has a purpose, including fear. Fear completely paralyzes us mentally and physically; it keeps us in a state of mediocrity. With fear in our heart, who we *think* we are and who we *know* we are in constant conflict.

Every time I reflect on a situation that caused me to be afraid, fear affected me physically, mentally and emotionally. My heart raced; I didn't eat or sleep. Sometimes I made every effort to ignore the situation hoping it would go away on its own. Fear made surrendering and complacency easy. Fear grabbed the little faith I had and choked the hope out of it.

As I matured in life, I learned not to allow my emotions or situations to dictate my faith. My faith had to become unchangeable in certain as well as the uncertain times. Fear and faith require the same amount of energy; one of them simply has adverse effects on our health [emotionally, spiritually, and physically].

Today, I consider myself a fear chaser because the things that used to send me running scared, I face head on with the confidence that God has my back. I keep it moving, in faith, with sweaty palms, a racing heart, and sometimes a trembling voice, *I go in faith*. I speak and expect everything that I meditate on and say to come to fruition. If they don't, I still do not worry because God knows what's best for me, and He always has my best interest at heart. I face challenges with prayer padded in faith. I chase fear out of my life by intercepting every negative thought with a positive one.

God's reputation is never questionable–only our faith *in Him* to do what we consider is too difficult or impossible.

I love the story about the Widow of Zarephath found in I Kings 17 starting at verse nine (NIV). When I read it, the widow's behavior reminded me of myself during one of my pitstop experiences. In the story, God sent Elijah on an assignment and gave him specific instructions. However, it was both Elijah and the widow's obedience that birthed long-term blessings. Although Elijah's purpose increased her faith by challenging her obedience; he, too, had to stretch his faith when the widow's son died. Whenever God sends us on a mission, expect the unexpected– expect to be tested.

Here's the conversation between God, Elijah and the widow:

⁹ "Go at once to Zarephath in the region of Sidon and stay there. I have directed a widow there to supply you with food." ¹⁰ So he went to Zarephath. When he came to the town gate, a widow was there gathering sticks. He called to her and asked, "Would you bring me a little water in a jar so I may have a drink?" ¹¹ As she was going to get it, he called, "And bring me, please, a piece of bread."

¹² "As surely as the LORD your God lives," she replied, "I don't have any bread—only a handful of flour in a jar and a little olive oil in a jug. I am gathering a few sticks to take home and make a meal for myself and my son, that we may eat it—and die."

¹³ Elijah said to her, "Don't be afraid. Go home and do as you have said. But first make a small loaf of bread for me from what you have and bring it to me, and then make something for yourself and your son. ¹⁴ For this is what the LORD, the God of Israel, says: 'The jar of flour will not be used up and the jug of oil will not run dry until the day the LORD sends rain on the land.'"

[15] She went away and did as Elijah had told her. So there was food every day for Elijah and for the woman and her family. [16] For the jar of flour was not used up and the jug of oil did not run dry, in keeping with the word of the LORD spoken by Elijah.

[17] Some time later the son of the woman who owned the house became ill. He grew worse and worse, and finally stopped breathing. [18] She said to Elijah, "What do you have against me, man of God? Did you come to remind me of my sin and kill my son?"

[19] "Give me your son," Elijah replied. He took him from her arms, carried him to the upper room where he was staying, and laid him on his bed. [20] Then he cried out to the LORD, "LORD my God, have you brought tragedy even on this widow I am staying with, by causing her son to die?" [21] Then he stretched himself out on the boy three times and cried out to the LORD, "LORD my God, let this boy's life return to him!"

[22] The LORD heard Elijah's cry, and the boy's life returned to him, and he lived. [23] Elijah picked up the child and carried him down from the room into the house. He gave him to his mother and said, "Look, your son is alive!"

[24] Then the woman said to Elijah, "Now I know that you are a man of God and that the word of the LORD from your mouth is the truth."

Keep in mind that the God's reputation is never on the line, just our faith in *choosing* to trust him.

> *"Mediocre faith produces mediocre blessings; mustard seed faith produces mountain-sized blessings."*
>
> *~Kandra C. Albury*

Fear shows up when faced with a decision like many of the ones below:

- Finishing or going back to school;
- Overcoming an addiction;
- Standing up for yourself or others;
- Exposing an abuser;
- Starting a business;
- Going to the doctor or dentist;
- Dating;
- Marriage or marriage after divorce;
- Starting a family;
- Being single;
- Dying or dying alone;
- Applying for a new job or changing careers;
- Learning to swim;
- Trying a different food;

- Flying in an airplane;

- Losing someone you love;

- Losing your home;

- Car repossession;

- Running for office;

- Rejection;

- Sharing your sexual orientation with family or friends;

- Losing a job; or doing something you've never done before!

- Many of these have been fears of mine or I've witnessed others deal with them.

When my husband and I celebrated our sixth wedding anniversary, we went on a cruise. I noticed a rock-climbing wall and told myself that I'd climb it before our trip ended. One day while on the upper deck, I looked at the wall and told James that I was going to climb it. He wasn't so sure about me climbing it so he reluctantly said OK and asked if I was sure I wanted to do it.

The timing was perfect because no one was in line and no one was around to see me make a fool of myself if it didn't go over well. I put on the harness, helmet and started climbing. I knew nothing about rock climbing, but I knew I was going to do it. The assistant guided me as I made my way up to ring the bell. At times, I wanted to quit but *something* wouldn't let me. Each step that took to reach the next level, I named it one of the things that I had conquered in life: divorce, abuse, debt, sadness, depression, bitterness, unforgiveness, lack, and suicidal thoughts. When I got to the top I rang the bell, it was one of the most victorious sounds I had ever heard in my life! A crowd had formed and applauded my efforts. It was a triumphant day for me!

Fear will cause us to talk ourselves out of our God-ordained blessing! Creflo Dollar once said, "we must hire faith and fire fear." Once you've been scared enough you become desensitized to fearing certain things. There are still some situations that frighten me, but not many. Prayer padded with faith and wisdom makes the unthinkable thinkable, the impossible possible, and the fearful, fear-less! Remember, God hears us… and all we must do *is ask*!

"If you have the guts to ask God, he has the grace to grant it! Let's hope you can handle it (whatever IT is). Got guts?"

~Kandra C. Albury

Say this with me: "I got grace, guts, and patience!"

Chapter Fourteen

Angels: Heaven's Ambassadors on Earthly Assignments

God uses people to speak into our lives. Their words should empower, confirm, reaffirm, and admonish (in a constructive manner).

When I moved to Jacksonville, FL. in 2000, I was a single mom enduring my divorce. I was hired as a television news producer with one of the stations. I loved it but working the night shift wasn't conducive for *this* single mom. Therefore, I searched for other employment opportunities. One of the places I went for an interview was at a call center that booked travel arrangements for executives across the country.

I arrived early for my interview and an executive called me in about 10 minutes after I arrived. He was nicely dressed and before he could get into the interview good, he introduced himself as Todney. He told me that I was not supposed to be there and that my children's college education was paid in full. At that time my girls were six and eight. I really needed a job and wasn't in the mood to hear what was down the road. I left and always remembered his name because he specifically said his name was like Rodney, but with a T.

Ten years later, in 2011, while working at an academic medical center in corporate communications, a coworker and I were waiting for the shuttle to take us across the street for lunch. She was conversing with a young lady about her newborn baby. I asked the young lady if she had a boy or girl, and she said a boy that she named after his father, *Todney*. My spirit leapt. Two days prior to our encounter, my husband shared with me that his employer would cover both of the girls' tuition as long as he stayed employed with the state college.

The next day I saw the young lady again, sitting on a bench outside of our building. Curiously, yet calmly I asked her a little bit about her husband's work history… she called him and said he remembered me. I told her that he told me 10 years ago that my children's college education was paid for and I didn't have to worry about that. We smiled and she said, "God always has a way of confirming his promises." It was during my oldest daughter's senior year, that God allowed me to reconnect with Todney and confirm his words.

Even when my girls waivered in school, I told them that a man of God said their college education was paid in full. I held on to his words until what he spoke came to pass.

Expanding *your* blessing capacity

Blessings require that we have the capacity to perceive them, receive them, appreciate them, and share them. We were created to pay it forward and reap the benefits of our gifts while impacting the lives of others.

In 2004, one of heaven's ambassadors spoke to James and I, while we strolled the neighborhood track. She said the Lord would give us a son. At the time we were engaged and hadn't discussed having children. We thanked her and continued exercising.

Four years later, in 2008, James and I expected our first child. Around the fourth month, something went terribly wrong and we lost our first baby boy. The date was October 26. It traumatized for me because I had never lost a child. I thought you got pregnant and had the baby– that's how it happened with my girls. I had a conversation with God and said, "I know You were supposed to bless us with a son, but not a dead one. I *will* believe *you* God, for a living, happy, and healthy son."

It was difficult for James because it was something he had looked forward to for a long time.

When we arrived home from the hospital, I asked James to turn the TV to Oprah. I knew if anyone could encourage my heart, she would.

The show was about a couple who lost their baby boy. He was born with a life-threatening illness. The doctors gave him a couple of months to live but he lived beyond what doctors expected. They released balloons in honor of his life. A short while later God blessed them with beautiful baby girl. I cried my eyes out. I said to God that if you did it for them, I know you'll do it for us.

I met with my doctor who said a large fibroid tumor caused the premature delivery of David Michael Albury. She advised that I have it removed via an open myomectomy and try again in six months. She didn't guarantee anything, but said it was worth trying. I went in for the surgery early on a Tuesday morning in April 2009.

A chaplain pulled back the curtain and asked if I wanted prayer. I was thought, "Lord, she would show up after I signed all the paperwork about the things that could possibly go wrong." I agreed to prayer; then the tall, black woman with bushy, curly hair said a short, sweet prayer then smiled and squeezed my hand. James and I had already prayed but the extra prayer couldn't hurt. The last thing I remember was being wheeled into surgery.

After waiting six months, in January 2009 we learned that we were expecting. It wasn't an easy pregnancy. There were times that I could hardly breathe, my heart would race after eating or just by walking around the house, but it was all worth it. On September 6, 2010 (Labor Day) Bryce Alexander was born. He was perfect and alive. God delivered on the promise because we kept the faith during one of our darkest pits.

A year later, I encountered the same chaplain on the elevator as I left work. I remembered her hair and I my eyes twinkled at her with excitement. When we arrived on the first floor, I stopped her and told her that she prayed for my husband and I before I had a surgery that would help us get pregnant. I pulled out my phone and showed her pictures of Bryce. Our eyes swelled with tears and we embraced. The moment was amazingly heartwarming!

I still can't believe that I had the audacity to tell God I wouldn't lead the dance ministry at my church, or ever dance again because *He* took *my* son. I was embarrassed and upset. I felt as if God had failed me, but after a while forgiveness settled in my heart and I returned to leading the dance ministry and dancing more passionately than ever before. I knew I could not just attend church and warm a pew with such an amazing gift and passion to dance. It was a gift God gave me without any formal training. While in *this* pit I discovered peace, productivity, and the promise of another son.

"When we neglect our prayer life, we find ourselves on one of life's merry-go-rounds, wondering when the ride will end. It ends when we kiss our past goodbye and wave as it inevitably fades into the distance."

~Kandra C. Albury

A legacy of faith, hope, love and contentment

Prayer requires us to acknowledge God as being *the* ultimate source [not an additional resource]; our careers, spouses or *special* connections don't sustain us – God does. When we practice the principal of writing down our dreams and praying (let's call it *journaling* the journey), it places our vision before us. Once we practice these principles, we position ourselves to experience divine release and favor. Not only are our needs met, but we will enter a realm of God's unwavering favor… *remember God **gives** us the desires that align with His word, everything that our hearts desire is already granted by God.*

My grandparents were some content folks because they learned how to "make do" but they also operated in three biblical principles: love, giving, and faith.

The more they shared, the more they were blessed to give. My grandfather delighted in growing vegetables and giving them away. Everything he grew was good! Whether it was greens, sugar cane, watermelons, oranges or tangerines… they were sweeter than honey and extra-large.

My grandfather was also a deacon who prayed the paint off the walls of Mt. Moriah Baptist Church in Hastings, FL. He often opened the service with a hymn.

My favorite hymn was:

"What a friend we have in Jesus all our sins and griefs to bear, what a privilege it is to carry everything to God in prayer. Oh what peace we often forfeit, oh what needless pain we bear all because we do not carry everything to God in payer."

While leading this hymn, the church mothers swayed from side to side, waved their fans in the air, and tears ran down their cheeks. I was a little girl and couldn't quite grasp what was really going on, but I knew whatever was going on was great and the God they sang about and praised had to be something special!

However, I quickly learned that there were conflicts on the deacon board, mother's board, also in choir number one, two, and three. Thus, I concluded that the experience was limited to a "church" lifestyle versus a true relationship with God. The more I attended church as a youngster and teenager, the more I realized that I enjoyed a good time but wanted to impact lives beyond the usual "high time" experience. I didn't want to just attend church and overhear gossip two days later about a deacon's wandering eyes or a missionary's daughter out-of-wedlock pregnancy; I wanted God's word to penetrate my life and change me, so I could inspire others. I wanted a Psalm 34:13-15 experience. I had been "churched" all my life—the Baptist way and the Pentecostal way… I was in pursuit of God's way once and for all.

I knew the order of service by heart: one fast song, one slow song, lengthy testimonies, offering, and the sermon; alter call, announcements, then finally the benediction. All of the kids had to memorize Easter and Christmas speeches. On top of that, there were programs galore, pastor anniversaries, usher board and choir anniversaries that included the same people leading songs (off key most of the time) in hot robes. Not to mention some of the people were rude and plain old mean and bitter, particularly those who "guarded" the kitchen.

At my childhood church, women and men sat on separate sides. We washed feet during communion and held tarry services… a service that *required* the saints to call on Jesus until their mouths foamed. I refer to my childhood church as the church of "cant's" because women couldn't wear pants, shorts, or makeup. We couldn't eat pork, grapes, or drink grape juice. Unsurprisingly, I started a quest to find a church of "cans…" one that promoted a personal relationship with God and not religious platitudes. As soon as I graduated high school, I left my childhood church on a journey of spiritual freedom and a leader who taught the benefits of righteous living. Fortunately, it didn't take long because I stopped waiting to hear a word from the pulpit, and I studied the word of God for myself.

"A kingdom lifestyle is living our best life by recognizing there isn't a need or desire too great or too small that God cannot fulfill– as long as the things we are praying for equip us to be more effective children of God."

~Kandra C. Albury

Chapter Fifteen

Are You Kingdom-minded, Double-minded, or Absent-minded?

A kingdom mindset is an expanded mindset. When you're kingdom-focused you're flexible and available to be used by God... anywhere, anytime, and under any circumstance or condition.

In July 2010, I was about eight months pregnant with my son Bryce; I waddled down to McDonalds for the Wednesday special... 69¢ cheeseburgers; I purchased two (one for me and one for Bryce). I also ordered two small fries, two apple pies (two for me, none for Bryce) and an orange drink. I had my mind set on those golden arches, which I could see from my 10th-floor office window. I put on my flats and started on the two-block hike up the street. The lines were unusually long for 11 a.m. It was hot, I was as big as a house, hungry, and ready to wrap my mouth around one of my all-time guilty pleasures. They finally took my order and I headed back to the office armed with my lunch. As I walked down the sidewalk, I saw a homeless man approaching me. I had already told to myself that I was not giving him my food; I didn't care how he asked because *I* was hungry, and sharing was not on my agenda! He got about three feet from me and said, "Excuse me, ma'am, I am hungry do you have anything to eat?" I was aggravated, but I immediately relented. I gave him Bryce's cheeseburger and one of my apple pies. To see him jump in the air and click his heels like he had won a million dollars did my heart and soul good!

If we are flexible and available, God will use us in whatever state we're in because Kingdom-minded people clearly understand that we were created for God's glory... and any time *is* a good time to be used by God (Hebrews 13:2)!

Moreover, kingdom-minded individuals *are not* double-minded, narrow-minded, carnal-minded or absent-minded. Kingdom-minded people are present, conscious, honest, and willing to take their thought processes beyond the familiar... and venture into the unfamiliar, unseen, and even unimaginable. It requires taking inventory then moving far away from negative energy, negative people, warped belief systems, and things that limit our mobility... physically and spiritually. We gravitate towards the imaginative, innovative and possible. As a result, we move closer to God and embrace His will for our lives. This requires much prayer and meditation that train our brain to tap into the supernatural. Time with God in prayer teaches us to be sensitive to His voice; and it disciplines us to act upon hearing it.

What I like most about kingdom-minded people is they know how to celebrate the accomplishments and blessings of others. They know they *are* good enough, they make the cut, and they are among God's elite warriors. They understand there are countless blessings to go around and plenty of room for others to walk in the blessing factor. They are not easily intimidated, jealous, or spiteful… they simply get it. They understand they are not an afterthought but a forethought and are always on God's mind. They teach and remain teachable and are not haughty or boastful. They help usher others into their destiny by sharing their life lessons and truths. In a room filled with people they don't have to say a word. Titles or status don't define them. They are grounded by the important things in life and walk in humility. They understand that their vision and purpose are bigger than themselves and must involve aiding others. Their mission extends beyond Earth and into the heavens.

Most importantly, they understand they are not subject to the bondage of religious doctrine but the greatness of God's grace. They seek relationship, not religion, and choose freedom and forsake bondage. They don't judge because they recognize that they, too, are fallible beings striving for righteous living and divine connections. Kingdom-minded people understand there isn't distance or time when it comes to those they love. Whether the individual lives in Africa or around the corner, nothing separates their divine connection.

Lastly and most importantly, they know that the same greatness exemplified by world icons and leaders such as Mahatma Gandhi, Mother Teresa, the Pope, or Maya Angelou resides inside of them.

"When we acknowledge the rock and shoulders on which we stand, we'll never find ourselves standing alone."

~Kandra C. Albury

Now those who are not kingdom-minded, but absent-minded, are often uncomfortable in the presence of kingdom people. The problem is they've been exposed to a glimpse of your gifts and talents. For those who don't embrace or understand kingdom living, you are a threat— much like a double-barrel shotgun aimed at their insecurities and inadequacies. These individuals can come in the form of bosses, friends and, unfortunately, family members too.

Your role is to keep your light shining because you are *that* city that sits upon a hill. Do not dim your light under any condition; don't even think about putting it underneath a table. Their insecurities are not your issue [pray for them]; because, kingdom-minded people understand properly handling non-kingdom-minded people is a part of the test that must be passed to advance to the next kingdom assignment. Regardless of *their* issues, we must continually express kindness and love to those who lack a kingdom mentality— it's with loving kindness that we draw people to God. Even if we don't draw them, we can at least leave them in awe of God's power working through us *for* them... but by the Grace of God (smile, it is doable with God).

"How would we know God to be a healer or mender, if we've never been sick or broken?"

~Kandra C. Albury

For several years I endured severe shoulder pain. I went to the doctor countless times and they prescribed a plethora of pain medications. I'd take the medicine and dealt with the side effects they presented. I also took numerous anti-inflammatory medications. One day I told God, "I do not want to take pills to go to sleep, and pills when I wake up. I want to be free from the pain." Then the next day I went walking and I was still in pain. So, I told my left shoulder, "You must line up with your right counterpart. Ligaments, I speak free flow of blood, all inflammation must go." Three days later, I noticed something was different. I hadn't taken any pain pills and I wasn't in any pain. God had answered my prayer of healing once I got specific and *opened* my mouth. The adversary desires to keep us quiet and professing the wrong thing. When I claimed the shoulder pain, and believed I needed medicine to feel better, I owned the condition. Fatefully, when I spoke directly to my situation with authority, faith, and expectation, my healing manifested.

I was so excited about my healing that I wanted to share it on Facebook with my friends. The minute I got ready to type my post, fear showed its ugly head and unbelief spoke, "What if the pain comes back?" I immediately intercepted the "what if" with a thought of knowing that it wouldn't come back because I had been totally healed.

When Jesus healed the blind man by spitting on clay and touching his eyes, He wanted to make sure the man's eyesight was whole… but the man also wanted wholeness. Consequently, when Jesus asked him what he saw after the first touch, the blind man responded that he saw men walking like trees. Then Jesus touched him again and his vision was whole. The blind man could have settled for blurry vision, but wholeness was his yearning. We must truly desire complete healing so much so that when we still encounter pain after praying, we speak and declare healing until we are 110 percent healed.

"If you think waiting for Mr. Right is hard, think about picking up the pieces after Mr. Wrong is long gone."

~Kandra C. Albury

Chapter Sixteen

Sassy, Single, and Surely Worth Marrying

I will never forget my single-hood journey! The ups and downs, ins and outs, and all the uncertainty; therefore, single ladies are near and dear to my heart.

One day I conversed with an acquaintance and she told me how hard it was holding down the fort alone and making ends meet as a single mother. As soon as I chimed in to say that I understood, she interrupted and said, "But you're married and have help." I kindly interjected and said, "I haven't always been married."

I know what it is like to ride on fumes while your car is making strange noises with two or three checks floating around to cover utility bills and payday is still four days away. I know all too well what it's like to be a single mom running a household. Not to mention, I had seen first-hand what my Mom went through.

I knew what it was like hoping that a date would end with some potential of a long-term relationship as I had kissed my share of frogs. My single journey coupled with being a single mom left me with my share of unforgettable bruises, struggles, and battles I overcame. It also taught me not to judge my single sisters, but to pray for those who deeply desire a covenant life partner.

Below are some words of wisdom, based on my single journey to each of you. These words are from my heart to yours:

- Being single can sometimes be a vulnerable time, especially if you haven't taken time to reacquaint yourself with who you are first. Take time to know and love you.

- If you pull a trick or two to get him, it'll take a bag of tricks to keep him. The best way to a man's heart is being a woman who seeks after God's heart.

- Know your value and what you bring to the table in professional and personal relationships.

- Don't allow yourself to feel desperate while waiting for Mr. Right or you will end up with Mr. Wrong.

- Don't make a potentially good soul mate suffer because you haven't forgiven yourself and other.;

- If a relationship becomes violent or toxic, end it!

- Don't easily relinquish your power.

- Don't place your gifts and creativity on hold to pursue a relationship; it's important to continue operating in your gifts.

- Don't allow others to take you off course when it comes to operating in your gifts.

- Don't place your life in the hands of someone who doesn't value or appreciate it.

- Don't neglect prayer, mediation and reading the Bible and or other inspirational works.

- If you have children, don't introduce them to dates until the relationship is on a serious track, even then *protect* your children.

- Resist being the other woman! When you settle for second fiddle, you are played vicariously. Sometimes you must let go of what you believe is your "good thang" so that better and the best can transpire in your life.

- Don't bash your children's father; they don't need a narrator, commentator, or illustrator because the truth always prevails.

- Take your children to the library, to the voting precinct, an art museum, furniture stores, model homes; to church and to the bank.

- Don't forget to maintain balance; you can't be everything to everyone!

- Don't bite off more than you can chew; protect your character and your credit– pay cash when possible and shop for bargains.

- Don't ignore your conscience. "Trust in God with all your heart and lean not to your own understanding. In all your ways acknowledge Him and He shall direct your path" [Proverbs 3:5-6, KJV].

Remember, you must be willing to do almost anything, without compromising your morals and values or breaking the law, to take care of your children—most good mothers do… it comes with the territory!

We must get to a place where God is the *only* person we allow to rake us over the coals because he's the only one who can guarantee that we'll come out shiny as gold! It is only in Him that we discover our ability to love ourselves and others unconditionally without being led astray. We must listen to His soft whispers, then pray for obedience and strength to heed to His voice. God wants us to be a *Proverbs 31* woman.

Lastly, no one wants a renovation project. Who wants to pull into a car dealership to purchase what they believe is a new car, and later realize that the motor is from a 1979 Pinto? No one! This is why lawmakers implemented the National Lemon Law, which protects consumers from buying what they believed were decent cars and later discover the car was a broken-down piece of junk. Consider yourself a package deal that's not on clearance and has not been marked down! *You*, my sister, are a limited edition nestled safely on the display shelf, it takes someone who knows exactly what they *want* and *need* to know *you* are the perfect fit *for them*! Market yourself accordingly.

"If you don't know your value, others will gladly determine it for you. Be warned, it might be less than you thought or better than expected... you decide."

~Kandra C. Albury

Self-evaluation

On a scale of 1-10 (10 being the highest), how do you feel about yourself and overall success?

- Do you feel worthy of a life partner? Why/why not?

- How have you added value to yourself over the past 5-10 years?

- Are you a Pinto, BMW, Bentley or Aston Martin?

- Do you consider yourself healthy (emotionally and mentally)? Why or why not?

- How do you determine your self-worth?

- If you could change some things about yourself, what would they be? And why?

- How well do you manage money?

- What are your gifts and talents? How do you use them?

- What are your deep-rooted issues? How do you plan to address them?

- What is your marketing strategy? What does your billboard say about you?

- Are you anxious about being married? Is your biological clock ticking away?

- Have your earnestly prayed for a mate?

- Do you have ulterior motives? Would you marry for money, love or both?

- Are you satisfied with being single?

When I became content with being single, that's when God sent my life partner. I didn't say I was perfect and single, but I made every attempt to find balance and not perceive singleness as a disease, rather a short-term state of being. Nonetheless, it is when you become content with a grateful heart, windows of opportunity open. No ladies and gentlemen, I don't mean stop taking care of yourselves, either. I believe as you prepare for things to transpire (faith in motion), you *should* think about those things that often trip people up in relationships such as little secrets or dirty habits.

Decide on *your* non-negotiables upfront.

- What do you bring to the table? What should he/she bring to the table?

- Is it okay to date him/her if they going through a divorce? Why/why not?

- Is it okay if he/she has children from various women/men?

- Does it matter if he/she is overweight, smokes, drinks or occasionally uses drugs?

- What morals or values will be uncompromised?

- Is it okay if they are a different religion or race?

- What if he/she tells you that they have been in a same-sex relationship?

- Does education or job status matter?

- Ladies, is it OK if you make more money than him? Why or why not?

- What if he stays at home with his mom? What if you're still at home?

- What makes him/her marriage material?

- How long is too long to be engaged?

- What if he doesn't have transportation or a job (in transition)?

- What if every other word is a curse word?

- What if he/she is a single parent? Would you seriously consider raising the child/children as your own?

Make sure you examine and reexamine your motives

When I met James; I was finally in a place where I could at least consider a true friendship with a person of the opposite sex; he is my first "real" male friend. My only goal for the relationship was for us to be friends (with no strings attached) and to help him experience a closer relationship with God.

I strongly believe because I didn't use trickery or ulterior motives to get his attention, God presented us with the opportunity to connect on purpose and develop a lifelong, covenant relationship. For those of you who are single, I encourage you to explore the endless possibilities of love and to live in the *now*… by abandoning religious dogma and doctrine and open yourself to love.

Love is an emotion that presents itself to those desiring it. It doesn't see race, religion or other barriers that we as humans often surround ourselves with. James was born and raised Catholic; I was born and raised Pentecostal (and Baptist when I visited my grandparents). When I told some of the *religious* folk in my circle that we had been talking about marriage they said, "Girl, I know you're not going to marry him; how can two *walk* together unless they agree?"

It played out something like this... I invited him to my non-denominational church and he said he really enjoyed the sermons. Then I went to a couple of Catholic services. Not much for singing or loud music (unusually quiet), a whole lot of praying... oh the pipe organ was nice. There was a whole lot of praying... but it was okay with me, because I enjoy intimate moments with God. The priest had a great sense of humor and the messages were inspirational, *not* the fire and brimstone sermons I became accustom to as a little girl and teenager.

We kept attending each other's church every so often and then one day he said, he wanted to become a partner at my church. I was blown away! God had answered my prayers. After dating for a year, then being engaged for another year, we were married.

Truth is, I wouldn't have picked him out of a lineup but God always knows exactly what we need. I don't care if you think all the good men or women are taken, if you are open to the possibilities of love, God who is also love, *will* send you that special someone – whether from the shores of Asia or the beautiful beaches of Jamaica! God wants to fill the void in your life. He has someone designed with you in mind, just prepare yourself for his or her timely arrival!

"Man's 'no' is God's 'yes' to the best for your life, meaning God has your best interest at heart. After all, we are made in his image."

~Kandra C. Albury

Prayer for my single sisters:

Heavenly Father, I pray for my sisters (wives in waiting). I pray that forgiveness rests in her heart. I pray that a loving, discerning spirit guides her as she waits for her king. Lord, prepare her for a lifetime of marriage by giving her a humble, earnest heart to address her issues by freely casting her cares upon you. I pray that she begins to seek your guidance for what a good wife is and should be. I ask you Father to place women and couples in her life that will mentor her and model healthy and strong marriages. As she waits, encourage her heart and remove fear and feelings of worthlessness. Replace all negative thoughts and emotions with feelings of hope, worthiness, love and joy. I even pray that you prepare the king for his ordained encounter with his queen. Every pain and negative emotion associated with childhood experiences are dealt with and replaced with forgiveness, wisdom, and unconditional love. Give him a listening ear, humble spirit and a willingness to communicate. Teach them both how to love; work together as teammates; and honor and respect each other for years to come. Lastly, I pray that their marriage will be lifelong and strong. Their love will be a testimony of your amazing grace.

I believe you have heard this prayer and will fulfill every request mentioned and unmentioned. In your name I pray. Amen!

A prayer for a husband from the heart of a lady in waiting:
God prepare me as I wait for my life partner. Make me accountable and responsible to you first by always honoring truth. I pray that my soul mate is humble, brave, born again and balanced. He doesn't have to be perfect, but teachable. Allow him to be a leader who is fair, walks by faith and is quick to forgive. God, give him insight, foresight and initiative to lead. Allow him to be diligent and anxious for nothing. Give him a heart of prayer and let him pray with his family often. God, please place the right people around him and build his self-confidence. If he isn't marriage material now, God, you do a work in him, speak to his heart and give him an obedient and discerning spirit to know your voice when he hears it. Allow him to leave all childhood and negative behaviors in the past; behind your veil of forgiveness. Grant him freedom through you as his God, friend, deliver, provider, and comforter. Use his hands and all of his gifts for your glory. God, even reveal new gifts and talents to him that will bring income into our home and into the Kingdom. Teach us to be emotionally responsible—never to speak in anger, bitterness or jealousy but in love, kindness and genuine concern. Restore his spiritual, physical, and

emotional health. Allow him to make healthy choices regarding our family. Allow us to lead together, pray together, love together, and live a lifestyle of worship together. Design us for each other because you know exactly what is best for us. Allow us to recognize the king and queen within and to submit to your will for our lives for the rest of our lives. God, help me to prepare for his timely arrival by dealing with my past and present emotions, and those deeply rooted issues.

Help me to be a good steward over my finances and everything that I am responsible for. Teach us how to love, support and comfort each other as well as how to protect our marriage from outside pressures. Give me a seeing eye to recognize when he is weak and to always pray earnestly in the spirit.

Most importantly Lord, help me to feel worthy of my King's love and vice versa. I believe you have heard this prayer and will fulfill every request mentioned and unmentioned. In your name I pray. Amen!

"Understand yourself so that others can better understand you. Get over yourself so that others won't get over on you."

~Kandra C. Albury

Check yourself because you love yourself

"But if you remain in me and my words remain in you, you may ask for anything you want, and it will be granted! When you produce much fruit, you are my true disciples. This brings great glory to my Father." John 5:7-8, NLT

The Bible states that when we place our trust in man, we will surely be disappointed. We must trust God by engaging Him in our Earthly affairs. When we invite God into our space, He will lead us to trustworthy people who are worthy of our respect, love, energy, and presence. Yes, you *are* royalty and not everyone can walk into a king or queen's palace.

When I was single, I often battled with loneliness and masked all of my weaknesses with pious replies when people would ask me why I was single. I'd say, "Jesus is my husband" Or, "I don't need a man because God is supplying my needs." I had a "church" response for every situation until I had a reality check. Subconsciously, I knew I was a wreck because I had allowed others to have way too much influence and control in my life. I had lost my sense of self while I fulfilled the expectations of others. Then one day I had a Kumbaya meeting with myself.

I set some things in order, and I started working on myself from the inside out. I didn't want to attend another emotional church service where I went to church empty and left empty. Once again, I wanted to own God's truth and peace for my life. In fact, while on my evening strolls I began having some heart-to-heart conversations with God.

During this time, I casted all my cares upon Him. I started working on my outer appearance by implementing an intense walking regimen, reading daily devotionals, and taking care of my needs first. I whitened my teeth, cleaned my skin, and drank more water. I was on a quest for truth and discovery of who God ordained me to be. I wanted to make myself more marketable and my life more manageable.

Before my mini transformation, I felt like a rundown BMW with a Pinto engine. I needed to be complete, and I did not want things or someone else to make me complete…I needed an awakening. I knew before I could entertain the thought of a serious relationship, I needed to address some deeply rooted issues.

One of the first issues I addressed, was my perception regarding my singleness; it was not a disease! It was a *temporary* state of being. Secondly, I stopped allowing other people to define my worth… and lastly, I believed in the power of self by knowing that God created me to conquer! I addressed these issues, and because I yearned for truth God eventually revealed dormant issues to me.

Even as an adult, I realized the depth of one of my suppressed issues as James and I photographed a wedding. I broke down at the reception during the father-daughter dance. I stepped outside to regain my composure. I wasn't jealous, but wanted to know why I wasn't good enough to have my father dance with me on my wedding day. Shucks, I had been married twice and no father-daughter dance at either reception. It was a pain that I didn't know was there until I witnessed such an innocent, loving, and special time.

Once I recognized the pain, I prayed about it. God said to me, "I allowed you to marry a wonderful life partner who will be there to dance with you for the rest of your life as well as with your daughters on their big day. His father sees you as the daughter he never had. Kandra, I have given you double for your loss."

Therefore, we must count our blessings and position ourselves to break generational curses. When we are moved by the voice of God, He will not allow the things that we struggled with to become the struggles of our children.

This brings me to the subject of generational suffering. We must pray specific prayers to cancel the negative words, deeds, and rituals of our ancestors. If we don't, we will find ourselves battling the same issues or other problems that are counterproductive. We have to cancel them out by simply praying a prayer of cancellation:

"Father God, anything that has been assigned or attached to my life that comes to forfeit my peace, love, worth, self-confidence, prosperity and health, I call it out and stand with You, the God of the universe, in believing that this problem won't plague me, my siblings, my children, or future generations. Amen."

You *should* choose to be specific about the issues that you and your family have faced. God loves our transparency!

"Choosing happiness over joy can cause us to remain in a holding pattern as we wait to receive that new car, new life partner, new job, new home or those to "die for" new pair of shoes. Resist the holding pattern syndrome."

~Kandra C. Albury

Chapter Seventeen
Grace is Yours and You Don't Have to Ask for It

"Everybody can be great, because everybody can serve; you only need a heart full of grace."

~Dr. Martin Luther King, Jr.

I heard this quote by Martin Luther King one morning when pulling into the gas station on my way to work. I immediately asked God for the heart of grace just as Dr. King described.

A couple days later, I had a court date with my ex-husband to settle child support for my oldest daughter as she had turned 18.

We arrived at court, sat before a judge and answered several questions. After the judge made his final ruling, we both left and returned to Jacksonville. I knew he was sick and could tell he wasn't feeling well. As we headed out of the courtroom, I asked him what he was getting ready to do and he said that he was waiting for the bus to return to Jacksonville. I said,

"Well, since I'm headed that way, I'll give you a ride." It was an hour and a half drive to our destination. We talked about the girls, God, and his diet. I pulled into McDonalds and asked if he wanted something to eat and he said sure. He never gestured towards his wallet, so I assumed he didn't have money, but that was okay.

As we neared downtown Jacksonville, I asked where he wanted me to drop him off. I had seen him hanging out in front of one of the city's shelters, but I wasn't sure if he stayed there. Then he asked me to drop him off at a transitional housing facility for homeless men. I felt some relief knowing he wasn't sleeping on the streets. I was armed with a gift bag full of toiletries that the girls bought him for Christmas since they didn't hear from him on Christmas day. On top of the toiletries was a picture of the girls took at Christmas in a black frame. He looked at the photo and smiled. When I backed out the driveway, God said, "Kandra, that's the heart of grace that you asked for."

I later learned that he never stayed at the men's shelter because I went there looking for him after sitting in the emergency room with him a few weeks later. After he was discharged, he had me drop him off there once again. After I didn't hear from him in days, I stopped by there to check on him. The clerk at the window looked through the log of names and photos, and asked if I had the right name. Then she said they never had anyone by his name on the facility's roster. He always did have pride about himself and he didn't want me to know that he was homeless. When I spoke with him, I asked him where he was staying. He sighed and said City Rescue Mission, the same shelter my family served Christmas dinner at in 2009.

"Grace is like ordering a cheeseburger – it comes with cheese!"

~Kandra C. Albury

A delayed response will build your character or turn you into one.

"For you know that when your faith is tested, your endurance has a chance to grow. So, let it grow, for when your endurance is fully developed, you will be perfect and complete, needing nothing." James 1:3-4

God's "yes" may require a ninety-day (or longer) waiting period but remember if he gave you a "yes" then His answer is *still* yes. I remember James landing one of his most exciting jobs with a chain of fitness centers in Orange Park, FL. It was a dream of his to work for a fitness center, especially since he previously held the title of Mr. Gainesville and still spent a significant amount of time in the gym.

During the organization's interview process, James and I went inside of the facility and walked the indoor track in faith trusting God for the job. It was close by the house, so he didn't have to drive too far to work. The job didn't pay a lot so we weighed our options and decided on the job at the gym, which was close to the house…at least we didn't have to budget nearly as much for fuel.

He worked as the manager for a year and a half, and by the end the second year the company transferred him to the location closest to Jacksonville Beach. Eventually the company downsized and instead of James getting laid off, he decided to undergo training in sales. It was a nightmare because if members cancelled their membership it was deducted from James' paycheck. We were struggling. He was getting off late, losing weight and our bills were behind and stacking up.

Then one day he said he was quitting. I didn't take him too seriously because I "thought" I knew James well enough to know that he wouldn't quit a job without having another job lined up. One day I came home from work and he told me that he had put in his two weeks' notice. I didn't get mad but I was concerned seeing as I was going to be the only one bringing in an income. We talked about moving closer to his parents or back to Gainesville.

One evening I was online searching for jobs in Gainesville and came across a planetarium director position at Santa Fe College for James. He was thrilled; it was what he had always wanted to do, especially since he had majored in astronomy and minored in physics. It was his dream job! Eagerly, he applied and was called for an interview. This was in August 2009. He was interviewed by a panel of the college's leaders and the process took about two and a half hours. When he got out of the interview he called me, and I could hear the excitement in his voice.

Two days went by and we heard nothing. We prayed and fasted and believed God for that job for James. Two weeks went by and no word, then a month went by, no word. James worried more than I did because we heard nothing regarding the status of the position. His faith started to dwindle. Then finally after waiting two and a half months, the college called and offered James the position. This situation reminded me of Sarah and Abraham. God promised them a baby and it took several years, but they had a baby as promised. Just like Sarah wavered in her faith, so did James. However, Sarah's faith diminished so much that she made plans of her own to assist God with *His* promise of a baby by having her husband impregnate their servant.

Coming to a place of having unmovable faith in God entails "tree-like" endurance. If you've ever witnessed a car hitting a tree, the only thing missing from the tree is bark, but the car is mangled or wrapped completely around it.

The Bible tells us that we should be like a tree planted by a river of water (Psalm 1:3). I believe Christ represents the water and *He* waters our roots (the deeply rooted issues and our faith), which allows us to flourish by growing deeper and stronger in him. It is essential that we find our water source, get planted, and allow it to nurture our roots. Once we're planted spiritually, the living water becomes our inner strength, conscience, and enables us to become an invaluable resource to our family, friends, co-workers, and our community.

Remember the time(s)…

I recall James having family stay with us so that they could attend a relative's high school graduation. He didn't tell me until a couple of days prior to them coming. It was also a couple of days before my birthday and we discovered bedbugs in the guest room. Subsequently, we had the house exterminated and we cleaned the room from top to bottom. I was frustrated and we did not budget to put his cousin, her granddaughter, and her one-year-old son in a hotel.

I wanted to meet these people because I had never met before, so rode with him to pick up them up from the bus station. Upon my encounter with the younger cousin, I immediately noticed that she had a baby on her hip and was very pregnant. I didn't have time to prepare the house like I wanted and the guest room was a wreck from being sprayed, and all of the furniture was dissembled. When we dropped them off at the house, I turned around and ran out to Wal-Mart. I purchased a queen-sized air mattress and a couple of other household items and some quick-fix meals.

We set up the double-chamber mattress in the living room and put some of my best linen on it along with some brand-new pillows. The next day, they slept in and I was a bit aggravated that the mattress stayed inflated in the living room. On top of that they played on their laptops almost all day. I ended up staying home from work because I just didn't feel right leaving relatives that I hadn't met, and James hadn't seen in years in our home unattended.

Around 5 p.m. they started getting ready for the graduation, which I drove them to. I was very upset with my husband because after all… these were his relatives and he didn't plan accordingly. I just knew the minute they started drinking his milk, they'd be out the door but not even that caused him to shorten their stay. James loves his milk!

I became more and more agitated by the minute when out of nowhere, the Holy Spirit checked me. I quickly began thinking back to 2010 when I was pregnant with my son Bryce and how I felt at nine months— I didn't want to do anything but have that baby. At the very moment that I started to become more frustrated, God spoke to me and said three simple words, "That was you." I was speechless!

His expectant cousin was me 20 years ago. My oldest daughter was one and swinging on my hip and I was eight months pregnant with Myra. She was even in school trying to finish her college degree just like I was at her age. God made it easy for me to take the high road by reminding me of the road that I once traveled. So out of conviction I sat in silence, smiled, and continued being a gracious host with a grateful heart.

After chauffeuring them around during their three-day stay, I drove them to the bus station located in downtown Jacksonville. I was sad to see them go and gave them all hugs. Lesson learned: Don't be so quick to forget *where you came from*.

"Even in a dysfunctional state we must find a state of functionality. Regardless of the trauma, God wants you to persevere, find healing, wholeness and closure so that you can live your best <u>blessed</u> life!"

~Kandra C. Albury

Chapter Eighteen

It Happened to You, but Refuse to Allow It to Ruin You

Through the years I've learned that the truth can be ugly and it can hurt but most importantly, it can liberate us spiritually, mentally, physically, and emotionally. Many of the truths that I've discovered in life, I didn't always like or agree with but in the words of my 80-something year-old godmother, "keep on saying good morning" meaning, keep on living and you'll discover all sorts of truths.

Things will happen in our lives that appear to be unfavorable [initially], but as we get older we manage to recognize the benefit of the situation and embrace the possibilities of now. Sometimes the very thing(s) that we attempt to block out of our minds, cover up, lie about, or avoid at all costs, end up staring us square in our eyes. Ultimately, the "thing" can lead us to our purpose and into our destiny, *if* we allow it.

Should we survive the pain of the "thing" that we *believed* would wipe us out; was simply meant to inspire others and substantiate God's glory and purpose in our lives.

My final truth has been something that has warped my truth since I was a little girl. It's something that has made me; broken me; scarred me, shaped me, and now, *it* will finally free me. That *something* is sexual abuse I endured as child and I survived the trauma because I was taught to love and forgive early on in life.

As a little girl, I seldom felt safe around men. Strangest thing is, I felt that no girl was safe around men because of the things that I had gone through—I felt that men were not to be trusted period! From coping with inappropriate looks, jokes and stares to having to clinch my knees together to keep roaming hands out of my underwear. The beauty of my childhood and innocence was shrouded by people my mom thought were trustworthy. I remained silent for years, which made me extremely passive in almost all situations. Most importantly, I never wanted my mom to think she failed at parenting because she did so much right.

As a child, I did not feel pretty, and with light skin being *"in"* and dark skin being *"out,"* the abuse only made me feel uglier. It made me feel ashamed and used. When I was little, I strongly believed that the only opinions that really mattered where those of adults; only grownups had a voice and they were always right. All the lies and ugliness made it easy to give into my gut instinct, which told me no one, not even my mom, would believe me and I'd be getting adults in trouble.

Besides that, I didn't want to add additional stress to my mom's struggling. So, for more than 30 years, I remained silent about that part of my life. I only felt safe in the presence of other children and resorted to silence around adults.

The first time I was sexually abused

The first time I was abused, my mom was taking us to the lake in Pomona Park. We stopped by the convenience store for popsicles and mom grabbed a Pepsi. When she parked the car, we ran straight towards the lake with excitement. Momma yelled, "and you better behave yourselves!" We responded in unison, "yes ma'am" and never looked back. Once I got into the water, I could see momma leaning on the car watching us. Then this heavy-set white man offered to teach my sister and

I how to swim. He put his hands down my swimsuit and touched what was never given a name in our home. I immediately froze. I knew something wasn't right! I didn't know what to say or what to do. I wondered if he did the same thing to my older sister. I could see my mom and didn't know how to signal for help. Every time after that incident when I was touched "there" I froze. The abuse led me to live my life in a frozen state. I was shocked beyond words for almost 30 something years, I would remain somewhat voiceless until I discovered the power of writing and my superpower–courage.

With the exception of the fat, white man at the lake, most my perpetrators, were people no one *would* have suspected or imagined, and if the abuse hadn't happened to me, I would not believe it either. My God mother's dad name John was another perpetrator. He had spent several years in prison for murder and when he was released, he stayed with my godparents. My fun times at my godparents turned into nightmares and no one even noticed. He had porn posters plastered on the walls of his bedroom that I could clearly see when the door would open and close. He'd sit by the window in the dinning room and when I'd head to the bathroom, he'd grab me by one arm, tongue kiss me and fondle me. I didn't know how to say

STOP to an adult. When he'd hear someone come he'd push me away. I hated him! I eventually started using the bathroom under the house (like a dog), which sat up on bricks so that I wouldn't have to walk past him. He was very old and always wore these farty-looking shorts and open-toe slides. His fingernails and toenails looked like those of a very old gopher–just nasty! He didn't have any teeth and smoked Newport cigarettes. He has prickly salt'n pepper beard with matching salt'n pepper hair. His stomach hang way over his shorts and he was very dark skinned with red eyes. He looked like the devil himself! I remember when he died, I was like "good" God will get him now for messing with me! People were crying, including my godmother... I didn't shed a tear. The funeral was held at the funeral home in Crescent City. There wasn't 20 people in attendance. That says a lot about the life he lived–creeper!

There were others too. The acts are not a figment of my imagination. I have not forgotten because the same gut feeling that told me no one would believe me, now tells me I'm believable, unstoppable, and undefeatable. The hidden abuse grew inside me like a tumor... I felt it and it was *always* there like a thorn in my flesh. Even when I made every attempt to block the episodes out of my mind, something triggered the dark memories… be it the news, a scene from a movie, a conversation, or a certain smell, especially burning trash.

The pain and hurt retightened its grip again when my daughter disclosed the abuse she experienced at the hands of her father. I had no other choice, except to confront it! I knew that I couldn't just passively survive abuse; I had to conquer it, master it, and defy the odds by reclaiming my true value, worth and beauty…my wholeness and my daughter's wholeness.

I've gone to my abuser's graves talked, and spat on headstones. I have also elected to forgive my violators. It wasn't easy but forgiveness has come. I even have compassion for perpetrators. Hate is to heavy of an emotion to bare, especially when you know God loves all of us even the perpetrators.

I dedicate this final chapter to those who chose to suffer in silence, for the sake of keeping the family "together," but choose a victorious attitude without confronting their violators. I also dedicate this chapter to my daughters Drea and Myra who have experienced abuse firsthand and know all too well the painful effects of it.

I would like to bestow the acrostic below to those who have suffered and continue to suffer in silence:

Acknowledge that it is not your fault.

Beneath the pain there's beauty, boldness and a butterfly longing to be free.

Unjust, ugly and unfair–that's what abuse is!

Silence your violators by speaking out and forgiving. Don't allow abuse to suck the life out of you.

Emerge from the pain and betrayal stronger and more determined to protect yourself and others.

I believe we can all identify with having the life knocked out of us. No, I'm not talking about a backhand smack that your mom or grandma gave you for being flippant or "talking back." I'm talking pain resulting from something that transpired that almost left you lifeless; it may have been a divorce, death of a loved one, or some other unfortunate life events. Eventually we all experience a place of lows that teach us to be thankful during our highs.

In 2007, I experienced a low of lows when my daughter who was about 13-years-old told me that her father had been touching her inappropriately. I was angry and shocked because as much as he and I had our differences, I never would have guessed that he would have violated our daughter, and because he violated her, he violated me!

Several days after she shared what happened, my mouth remained parched and I lost my voice. I had not been to a concert or sporting event but the pain silenced me just like it did when I was a little girl. I lost my appetite and was completely numb. I cut off almost all communication and kept a straight face for work and in front of my girls; I tried to make everything seem normal. I'd break down on my drive to and from work and while I bathed. Those were the only times that I allowed myself to be real with myself. I wanted to kill the girls' father but couldn't because I did not want someone else to raise my girls while I served a life sentence for murder.

My daughter thought the world of her father, the sun rose and set on him and vice versa. As a result of the abuse, it sent her into a tail spin. She started stealing and being promiscuous. It was the longest, darkest season of my life. Emotionally and spiritually, I withstood hurricane force winds and rain.

However, when the skies cleared, my mind and soul were still intact, thank God!

My daughter told me that she wanted to confront her father, something I never had the courage to do. This was a sign to me that I had raised her to have a voice and that her voice mattered.

One Sunday after church, we drove to his residence. I sat next to her and held her hand while she interrogated her father. He adamantly denied it! She walked towards the door with tears streaming down her face. I turned to him and shook my head in disgust. We got in the car and I rubbed her hand and headed home. I told her, "If he never admits it, you know what happened, you confronted him, and the last step is finding forgiveness."

I realized that she was stronger than I ever was because I chose to forgive and not confront. To this day, her strength amazes me. I've always encouraged her not to let what happened to her to ruin her. I can tell she's still angry with her father. I pray someday she'll forgive him.

After this incident, I told her father that nothing good would come of him until he did right by owning his actions and sincerely apologizing to our daughter.

A year after counseling and dealing with her acting out, prosecutors contacted me and said they were ready to move forward with the case. I was frustrated and couldn't figure out why the legal process had taken so long. I called a friend who worked for the Department of Children and Families and asked her to share her thoughts. We were reading from the same sheet of music. At a time that my daughter was starting to regain some sense of normalcy. State officials wanted to prosecute her father, which would undo the counseling and progress that had been made. So, I prayed and informed them that she would not be testifying against him.

The day that I decided not to allow my daughter to testify was the day that I said yes to allowing God's vengeance to prevail. God's justice is swift, and in my granny's voice, "God is a just God all by himself."

In 2009, he ended up in the hospital where I worked, severely ill. He had been there for a month and I wasn't aware of this until I received a phone call from one of his brothers who informed me of his failing health. From the sound of his voice, the situation was serious.

We jumped in the car and headed to the hospital around 8 p.m. He was emaciated and didn't look like himself. He had gone from more than 200 pounds down to 145 pounds. I believe we all felt sorry for him. My husband anointed all of our heads and we joined hands and prayed. His skin was extremely dry so the girls put lotion on his legs and arms. That same night, we took his dirty clothes home; we washed, dried, and folded them.

Almost every day for two months, I called or visited him on my lunch break. I brought him a snack before leaving for the day. Outside of asking how he was doing, or if the doctor had stopped by, our conversations were minimal.

One day when I went to visit him he asked if I could assist him with filling out his paperwork for social security benefits. I agreed and the next day I picked up the paper work and started the tedious process of completing the forms. I came across a question where all dependents had to be listed. I couldn't believe it! So, I added the girls' information first. Little did I know, that in a matter of a few months they would receive a social security disability benefit as well as child support! Their ship had finally arrived [look at God, *just kidding*]!

Then a few days later, I received a call at work, it was my ex-husband saying, "I'm sorry for everything." I told him it was okay, and he should focus on getting better. I had already forgiven him, and my anger, pain, and bitterness had transformed into compassion.

I later learned that his parents' house, which was left to him by his mom when she died, had been turned over to the county for delinquent taxes. Someone in the area purchased the house and bulldozed it.

I couldn't help but think that God wouldn't allow the place where the abuse happened to remain standing; there was evil in that house! My daughter will never be able to drive by the house or enter it again.

His health was failing, he was unemployed, and he was homeless. Even to this day, I cannot bring myself to say he got what he deserved because the truth is none of us could handle what we truly deserve for our past or present wrongdoings.

My daughter managed to graduate high school, become a debutante, and receive the Dothea Smith President's award. It was very fitting for my daughter to receive this prestigious award as Mrs. Smith is an icon in her community. My daughter danced with my husband and it seemed as if at that moment, time stopped, and her journey of healing and wholeness began. She was accepted into college and worked part-time as a sales consultant at a bridal shop. In December 2018, she graduated from the University of Florida. We're a family of Gators!

I am so thankful to God that the trauma didn't ruin her but inspired her to one day open a shelter for girls called "Saving Grace." She plans to teach other girls how to overcome tragedy with triumph. Her long-term goal is to become a prosecutor in which she will prosecute those who commit acts of sexual abuse and domestic violence.

I learned through various trials to count my blessings even during my rainy seasons because once the skies clear, I realized that God was there carrying me, high above His head cradled in His arms, close to heaven. Although many times I could not sense Him, feel Him, or hear Him, I chose to believe in Him… especially during my pitstops. Now, pitstops and destinations are not the same, regardless of how similar they make look or feel. You must decide whether something is designed for a short stay (pitstop) or a prolonged visit (destination). It is up to you to determine the length of time you want to stay in a situation; whether you will *conquer* it or allow *it* to conquer you.

If I allowed my past situations to be my *final* destination, I would have never had the ambition to accomplish so much in life, including writing this book.

I applied the following principles to defy the odds and master my situations:

- Speaking and believing the positive.

- Abiding in love and allowing it to overtake every negative emotion.

- Praying daily.

- Writing a vision for my life (include the bells and whistles), you may get the bells if you don't get the whistles.

- Fasting (if you don't understand the purpose, consult the two G's (God and Google).

- Forgiving; it's good for the past, present, and the future.

- Challenging my gut, particularly when my situations were haunting.

Even in a dysfunctional state we must find a way to function without being reckless or irresponsible. Believe it or not, God is rooting for us and He wants us to persevere; find healing so that we can live our absolute best and blessed life… starting today!

Remember, because we belong to the most-high God, we were created to conquer, equipped to master, and destined to defy the odds!

Say THIS: "Because I am a child of the most-high God, I am created to conquer, made to master, and born to beat the odds!"

Chapter Nineteen

From the Shore

After that awful incident at the lake, I was shocked beyond words for almost 30-something years. I would remain somewhat voiceless until I discovered the power of writing and my superpower–courage.

My mom taught us how to survive, be respectful, and honest, but not how to protect ourselves from predators. Courageous conversations didn't happen in our home, which explained why sex or sexual abuse seemed like something that just happened. Now there were those occasional warnings to my sisters and I about staying away from boys because "they'd give us a baby" we never discussed body parts and why they shouldn't be touched. Unfortunately, for me, it wasn't the boys I had to worry about; it was the grown men that I just couldn't seem to avoid.

My encounters with sexual abuse happened between the ages of 5-7. I say between because I can't remember exactly how old I was when the horrendous acts occurred. Except for the man at the lake, my mom *knew* all my predators. No, she didn't know what happened to me because I didn't have the words to describe the violations or the courage to tell her. I was at a complete loss for words.

In fact, 60 percent of children are abused by someone their family knows and trusts, while 90 percent of children know their abuser.

As a little girl, the abuse *almost* left me hopeless. I went from happy, bubbly, giggly and goofy… to numb, sad, and aloof; particularly around adults. I became a mute and would only feel comfortable talking around other children. The ounce of hope that I found really was in going to church because attending church, regularly, wasn't an option–it was a way of life. But I had a problem with the God of my childhood because I often wondered that if this God was so big, bad, and mighty, then why didn't He look out for me? Why didn't He just stop it? He could have sent a lightning bolt or something to get rid of those bad men. Did He turn His back on me or take a nap and totally miss what happened to me?

Then again, He is a God that never sleeps or slumbers, at least that's what my granny would say about Him. Well every time I was abused, I thought surely, He was napping, making butterflies, and painting rainbows in the sky.

The abuse *almost* took my voice. I mean it nearly crushed it… and when I became an adult, I didn't know how to speak in public. I didn't know how to place an order or make eye contact with people. Nevertheless, I loved watching the news, which would later become my passion as a television news reporter. Little did I know that the silence from the trauma was the preparation I needed for my indescribable journey as a children's advocate and author. Although my journey started out with sexual abuse, right after high school, I married into domestic violence. As a result, I wanted nothing to do with the God of my childhood or my early adult years because He just didn't seem to treat me right.

Finally, I realized that it wasn't God, some of it was my own fault and some of it was life in general. I failed to form a relationship with Him and receive His amazing grace as a responsible adult. But how do you become vulnerable with a God that allowed so many horrible things to *just* happen to you? Fortunately, one day I read Romans 8:28. It was merely ink on paper for a long time because I simply read the words...without meditating on it or truly believing it.

Then one day God spoke to me and said, "*I am not like man, let me in a little closer. I love you and will move heaven and earth for you.*" I cried profusely. I didn't think for years that God loved me because I was abused and He did nothing about it. I held a grudge against God, and I wouldn't let Him in all the way. I wanted to believe in Him just enough to make it into heaven...Totally forgetting that I can experience heaven on earth and because I had accepted Him into my heart, I was already heaven bound, but *bound* by my past.

Consequentially, I had an epiphany and I realized that I am *not* what happened to me, but I am what I *conquered*! The word affirms this by declaring that we're **more** than conquerors through Christ Jesus who loves us. It felt like I was "backing into" my relationship with God in my late 30s after being raised in the church all my life.

Nevertheless, I struggled with no self-esteem because it was lower than low, and my well was completely dry. I was extremely defensive and struggled with abandonment, rejection, poor body image, trusting people, and even trusting God. This was me, as a church-goer for years. I still blamed my dad for my abuse because he didn't stay with my mom to protect me. I was a ticking time bomb, and no one knew it… at least I hoped no one knew it. My brokenness was my *normal* and I hoped no one knew *that* either. My greatest weapon was my ability to discern and write so I took comfort with a journal or laptop. Because I wasn't a talker, I could discern the motives of people. Things began to work for my good.

In 2013, I worked as a speech writer in Corporate America. I had been in corporate settings for 12 years and I kept hitting a glass ceiling. So out of mere frustration, I asked

God, what's next because I could not continue writing speeches, press releases, media advisories, and running around like a chicken with my head cut off on the weekends while helping my husband photograph weddings. I was done. God spoke to me as I was driving across the Fuller Warren Bridge in Jacksonville, FL.

As I returned from my lunch break, tears streamed down my face. He said, "Write books." Me, I don't write books, I write speeches, press releases, media advisories, and feature stories, not books." Next thing I knew, there were crickets–dead silence. I heard nothing else. Then I said to God, if I write you will have to tell me what to write about. Then I heard "From Food Stamps to Favor." I told God if I write THAT then people will know my business. God said to me, "Don't be ashamed because I have always been with you." I completed my memoir in six months and my first children's book "Don't You Dare Touch Me There!" shortly thereafter. This is when I left my last corporate position and relocated to Gainesville with my husband of 12 years and our three children. Things started to happened and shift. But I was still fragile, yet, trusting God with this senseless idea of becoming an author…Or at least I thought it was senseless.

In 2015, a friend called me and told me about ReClaim Global in Jacksonville, FL. It is a no-cost, intensive program that offers healing to adult survivors of childhood sexual abuse. I called the number and little did I know that the same way Jesus met the woman at the well, He would meet me at ReClaim Global. I unpacked more emotional baggage in three days than I had done in my entire life, I became free INDEED! My life was forever changed. Healing is now my portion and I wear a cape…Oops, I meant a garment of praise as stated in Isaiah 61:3

"…To give them beauty for ashes, the oil of joy for mourning, the garment of praise for the heaviness; that they may be called tress of righteousness…"

I stand tall like the trees. I'm redeemed, not guilty, and righteous. I'm strong and courageous, but best of all, it all worked out for my good and for God's glory. Today, I'm an author and God's champion for children! A children's advocate who empowers children and adults with my literary works and COURAGEous Conversations ™. I am the founder of Kids'n Capes, Inc. a non-profit organization that specifically works to prevent and raise awareness of sexual abuse, bullying, and illegal drug use. I have read my signature book, "Don't You Dare Touch Me There", to more than 5,000 children and adults in Florida, Georgia, Colorado, and Texas and Kigali, Rwanda. *My Story—Garment of Praise* is currently airing on Trinity Broadcasting Network (TBN), the largest Christian Network in the world. Apparently, God never turned His back on me nor was He napping when those horrendous things happened to me as a child, He was making sure I was armed and COURAGEously ready to soar into my destiny; while working tirelessly to prevent and raise awareness of childhood sexual abuse! It all worked together for my good... and now my voice is heard from here to the heavens! God is and has always been my source, and courage is my superpower!

Chapter Twenty

Healing Prayer for Victims of Childhood Sexual Abuse

Father, in the name of Jesus, thank You for the spirit of this courageous conqueror of childhood sexual abuse and how she is still standing despite the deep-rooted pain she's endured. I speak to every place that has been violated in her life. Father, I pray against the perpetual feelings of guilt, shame and self-blame. I bind those feelings right now in the matchless name of Jesus. I loose a newfound sense of peace, freedom, wholeness and fearlessness.

The question of "Why did this have to happen to me?" will no longer torment her mind. I decree and declare she will step into the place of wholeness and declare that even the abuse will work for her good and for Your glory in Jesus' mighty name! The heaviness of the secret is no more. And according to (Isaiah 61: 1-3) You Lord, shall give her beauty for ashes, the oil of joy for mourning and a garment of praise for the spirit of heaviness. And according to Romans 8:28, we know all things work together for the good. And this childhood trauma, God, You will make good on your promise of healing. I'm expecting it and so it is! Depression and sadness shall be no more. I decree and declare abuse will not be an excuse to be bitter or to sabotage blessings. Father God, do not allow her past to haunt her because she is free, in the mighty name of Jesus. You are

Jehovah-Rophe, the God who heals and we believe this to be so!

Father God, may You heal this conqueror in such a special way that she will become an ambassador of change, courage and hope to other victims who have experienced the physical, mental and emotional scars of childhood sexual abuse. May she be led to share her testimony of healing and deliverance in due season! May conquerors arise in every nation to expose childhood sexual abuse and carry it through to justice. We are Your change agents designed to shift the paradigm from brokenness to wholeness, in Jesus' mighty name.

Plant Your courage ambassadors where You see the greatest needs, in Jesus' mighty name. Lord send her, and she will COURAGEously go! May we not rest, but remain vigilant on the wall. May You speak to our spirit and lead us in fervent prayers to end sexual abuse and sex trafficking of children. May this conqueror tear down the attacks of the enemy that sexual abuse desires to bring. Sexual abuse is an attack of the enemy designed to steal our born identity and expose our society to social ills such as teen pregnancy, illegal drug use, alcoholism, mental illness and sexual promiscuity. I decree that, in the realm of body safety, no weapon formed against me, or any child, shall prosper.

I pray Jeremiah 29:11 over this conqueror's life and it reads: "For I know the plans I have for you," declares the LORD, "plans to prosper you and not to harm you, plans to give you hope and a future. You created us to prosper and be in health, even as our souls prosper (3 John 1:2). May mental and emotional healing be this conqueror's portion. May she rise from the ashes of her past and walk boldly into her destiny as a new creation in Christ. Allow her life to be a picture of beauty and holiness. Send perverted thoughts she may have towards herself into the abyss; never to return. Teach her to love, trust and forgive. May she also forgive her predator and those responsible in Jesus mighty name we pray, amen.

Decree and declare this with me aloud:

1. I am not guilty.

2. It was not my fault.

3. I was completely mishandled as a child.

4. I didn't know what to say or what to do or how to explain what was happening to me because I did not have the vocabulary.

5. I release this guilt, shame and self-blame right now in the mighty name of Jesus.

6. Forgiveness does not mean reconciliation. I do not and will not expose myself to anyone who has cause me physical, mental and emotional harm in Jesus mighty name!

This powerful prayer is also featured in the:

Awesome Women On The Move: National Prayer Book...Praying for Everything Under the Sun

by Tenaria Drummond-Smith and 54 Co-Author Women.

A special note from the author:

I believe you are well on your way to complete healing. I believe if God healed me of childhood sexual abuse, He shall do even greater in you. And remember, He who has started a good work in you shall perform it until the day of Jesus Christ.

Also visit www.reclaimglobal.org for additional information regarding a no-cost program specifically for adult survivors of childhood sexual abuse and sexual trauma. Participants must be at least 18 and up at attend.

Dr. Kandra Albury is a conqueror of childhood sexual abuse. She is the author of the Feisty Four Children's Book series and a children's advocate. In addition, she is a certified Darkness to Light sexual abuse prevention training facilitator. She is a minister and is a member of Living Covenant Church in Alachua, FL.

She believes that healing is possible, however, survivors must pursue it through prayer and seek resources that are available to aid in the healing process.

About the Author
Kandra C. Albury

Kandra Albury was born and raised in Crescent City, Fla., and educated in the Putnam County School System. She is married to James C. Albury, and the proud mother of two beautiful, adult daughters, Drea and Myra. She also has a young, handsome son by the name of Bryce and a grandson Kenzy. She resides in Alachua, FL.

Kandra has a bachelor's degree in communications from the University of North Florida; a master's degree in mass communications from the University of Florida, and a Ph.D. in ministerial education from Truth Bible University.

Her literary and children's advocacy work has been featured in numerous print publications as well as on local, national and international television networks such as WCJB-TV-20, WUFT, WJXT-Channel 4, African Network Television-ANTV (host of the Kids'n Capes Show).

For more information about Kandra, visit: www.kandraalbury.org.

For more information about support services for adult survivors of childhood sexual abuse, visit www.reclaimglobal.org.

*"Life's growing pains can make you **feel** like you don't have purpose, or they **will** drive you to your purpose. I've chosen the **latter**!"*

~Kandra C. Albury

www.ingramcontent.com/pod-product-compliance
Lightning Source LLC
Chambersburg PA
CBHW020404080526
44584CB00014B/1165